GrowingBonsai Indoors

Pat Lucke Morris and Sigrun Wolff Saphire
Editors

BROOKLYN
BOTANIC
GARDEN

Elizabeth Peters
DIRECTOR OF
PUBLICATIONS

Sigrun Wolff Saphire
SENIOR EDITOR

Steve Clemants
SCIENCE EDITOR

Joni Blackburn
COPY EDITOR

Elizabeth Ennis
ART DIRECTOR

Scot Medbury
PRESIDENT

Elizabeth Scholtz
DIRECTOR
EMERITUS

Handbook #191

Copyright © 2008, 2011 by
Brooklyn Botanic Garden, Inc.

ISBN 978-1-889538-79-2

Printed in China by Oceanic Graphic Printing.

♻ Printed with soy-based inks on
postconsumer recycled paper.

Guides for a Greener Planet (formerly All-Region
Guides) are published by Brooklyn Botanic Garden,
1000 Washington Avenue, Brooklyn, NY 11225.

bbg.org/handbooks

Cover: A 50-year-old natal plum (*Carissa macrocarpa*), trained as a cascade-style bonsai.
Above: This *Serissa foetida*, trained as an informal upright, is just about three inches tall.

Growing Bonsai Indoors

Bonsai Moves Indoors

Pat Lucke Morris

Visit any of the great bonsai collections around the world, and you quickly come to understand that a large number of fabulous specimens like a cold climate. They are cold-temperate deciduous and evergreen trees native to northern lands and need a dormant period of cold and rest every year in order to lead a long and healthy life. That these temperate species should make up a great deal of the world's bonsai is not surprising, given that the art is traditionally considered an outdoor pursuit. In Japan, extremely low temperatures are rare beyond the northernmost regions, and the temperate trees popular for bonsai there live outdoors all year long.

Even though the art of bonsai has traditionally been practiced on hardy plants outdoors, since the middle of the last century, growing bonsai indoors has become increasingly popular. If you'd like to begin cultivating bonsai in your home but are not in the market for a cool greenhouse that can accommodate cold-hardy northern trees, the tropical and subtropical bonsai found in the southern U.S., most of South and Central America, Taiwan, southern China, Southeast Asia, and India are much more promising options to start with. In their native locales, these trees are also cultivated outdoors year-round. The fortunate bonsai artists in those balmy regions do not need special techniques for cultivating and protecting their creations. The good news for cold-climate bonsai enthusiasts is that it's quite easy to emulate the growing conditions for tropical and subtropical species, plus a number of warm-temperate species, inside the average house or apartment. Whether you wish to purchase your first bonsai and learn to nurture it or shape one yourself from a nursery plant, this book can start you on the path to bonsai artistry. But beware, bonsai can become a passion.

A Few Notes on the History of Bonsai

The beginnings of the art we know as bonsai trace back almost two thousand years. Its roots are visible in depictions of floral arrangements in early Chinese art dating to circa AD 200. These early floral and garden images already indicate a blending of horticultural

Tropical plants like Asian jasmine lend themselves to indoor bonsai. Styled as a cascade, the 23-inch-tall specimen on the facing page has been in training for 50 years.

skill with aesthetics to evoke the spirit of nature. The 17th-century Chinese text *The Mustard Seed Garden Manual of Painting*, with references to floral arts dating back to 495, is still useful and popular with contemporary bonsai artists and teachers.

The Japanese word *bonsai* translates as "to train in a tray." The term is *penjing* in China, where the art form has flourished and developed into a variety of schools, including landscape bonsai, in which elaborate displays are built with trees and stones combined to create landscapes in shallow trays. The Chinese representations of mountains and water in these landscapes often include tiny structures and figures of men and animals.

During the Tang dynasty (618 to 906), delegations of Japanese officials traveled to China, beginning an extensive exchange of arts and ideas that continued for centuries. In time, the Japanese developed bonsai styles and techniques suited to their own native plants and their distinctive artistic and cultural concepts.

Initially, all the trees that became bonsai had been formed and shaped by nature. As suitable, good-quality trees became more difficult to find, the Japanese devised techniques for growing and training bonsai from young plants. By the mid-19th century, they had refined the styles and techniques for bonsai training and codified the aesthetic principles. These rules still guide modern bonsai artists.

In the United States, the first bonsai artists were Japanese immigrants who had settled on the West Coast in the late 19th and early 20th centuries. Although a few early merchant ships to China had brought trees in containers to Great Britain and North America, these early imports were essentially curiosities and did not spark the interest that occurred later, perhaps because they lacked wide exposure.

At the end of World War II, American servicemen stationed in Japan were exposed to the art of bonsai, and many brought examples back home with them. (Chinese versions of bonsai and penjing reached the West later because of political upheaval and restrictions.) Since then, and with typically American exuberance, the art of bonsai has been embraced and extended to many species of American trees, including many tropical and semitropical species.

Bonsai at Brooklyn Botanic Garden

Brooklyn Botanic Garden's own bonsai collection started with 32 trees in 1925 and now numbers about 350 trees, encompassing hardy as well as tropical, subtropical, and warm-temperate species. Starting with the leadership of bonsai curator Frank Okamura, who was responsible for the collection from 1947 until his retirement in 1981, Brooklyn Botanic Garden has been at the forefront of popularizing bonsai for indoors and out. Realizing that many bonsai lovers were eager to grow dwarfed potted trees in their homes, Mr. Okamura started to experiment with nontraditional species suitable for indoor cultivation in the 1950s and taught widely on the subject. This current handbook follows in the steps of two BBG classics on the topic, published in 1976 and 1990, respectively. Each has been reprinted many times.

HOW TO PURCHASE A BONSAI

Pauline F. Muth

- **Select a species suitable for indoor growing.** Consider the light, temperature, and humidity in your home and select a species whose natural growing conditions match as nearly as possible. For indoor bonsai, avoid hardy deciduous trees like maples and hardy evergreens like junipers and pines.

- **Choose a style that you like.** Bonsai is an art form. It should please the owner's eye.

- **Assess the health of the tree.** The tree should have good color and vigor and be free of problems. Look out for physical damage and insect or fungal problems before you purchase a tree.

- **Check the quality of the pot.** It must have one or more holes and allow extremely good drainage.

- **Check the quality of the soil.** The tree should be potted in bonsai soil—not regular garden or potting soil. Bonsai soil allows proper aeration and drainage and facilitates root growth. The surface must have large areas of loose soil. Do not purchase a tree if the soil surface has been treated with glue or the soil is hard packed.

- **Note whether there is wire on the tree.** Wire is commonly used for shaping and will need to be removed sooner or later. You may personally do this or have the seller do it at the appropriate time. Make sure that the wire is removed before the tree grows into it and is damaged or scarred.

- **Ask the artist or vendor for particular instructions that apply to the bonsai you are buying.** Be sure to ask for the date of the tree's last transplant and when it should next be repotted.

Growing bonsai requires a long-term commitment. The mature European olive forest pictured here has been in training since 1972. It is 19 inches tall.

Bonsai Styles

Pauline F. Muth

Observe old trees in nature, and you will see plenty of variation. Trees grow upright or slanting, in groups, pairs, or alone, out on plains or clinging to the sides of mountains. They are found in arid, moist, hot, freezing, still, and windy environments, and everywhere in between. Wherever they grow, trees are also affected by animals and diseases. All the stresses that nature places on trees are reflected in their shapes. Bonsai artists look at what nature creates with these factors and work to emulate it when shaping a tree, but they also add their own vision to produce a beautiful bonsai. That's why a bonsai is so much more than just a tree in a container.

The Five Basic Styles

Bonsai styles can be grouped in many ways. Five basic forms derive their names from the tree's angle of growth from a container and provide a common starting point for exploring styles.

- **Formal upright, or *chokan*** The tree grows straight and vertical.

- **Informal upright, or *moyogi*** The tree grows vertically but has movement to its trunk line.

- **Slanting, or *shakan*** The tree leans to one side, but the top remains over the pot in which it is planted.

- **Semi-cascade, or *han-kengai*** The tree leans over the edge of the container.

- **Full cascade, or *kengai*** The tree leans over the edge of the container and cascades downward, often dropping below the bottom edge of the container.

All other styles of bonsai are modifications of these five basic styles.

This 100-year-old thyme has been trained in the semi-cascade style.

Formal Upright Style | *Chokan*

Most bonsai students begin to learn the structure of bonsai by creating a formal upright design, called *chokan* by the Japanese. Once you have mastered the basics of design with a formal upright, you will be able to design other styles more easily.

In its most basic form, this style depicts a single tree standing alone. It emulates a tree found in nature that has not been affected by the stresses of fierce winds or other trees growing close to it. Study old solitary trees in nature to help you visualize the style. As you progress in bonsai, you'll see that there are many variants of this style. Learning the rules of design for a formal upright tree will give you a grasp of all the other styles of bonsai. Learn the basic rules, and then later you can bend or break them to add originality to your designs.

Basic Design Rules

- The first thing you need to do when you start working with any tree is to look at it overall and decide what the front view will be.

- The trunk line should be straight, with the apex (the top of the tree) over the center of the trunk base, and must taper from base to apex.

- The roots should spread out from all sides of the trunk. (The term *nebari* is used to describe the spread root formation.) This helps create the illusion of old age.

- The first branch should be to the left or right of the trunk as viewed from the front of the tree. It is usually one-third of the way up from the base of the tree.

- Ideally, but not always possible, the second branch will be a back-growing branch that can be seen slightly from the front and help develop depth for the composition. Never style the first branch this way.

- The third branch will be opposite the first branch but at a slightly higher level.

- As you select branches from the bottom to the top, be sure of the following:

  –Each successive branch is, or appears to be, shorter than those below it.

  –The diameter of the branches decreases as they near the apex.

  –When viewed from the top, each branch gets sunlight.

  –The distance between branches decreases as they near the apex.

–The movement and angle of all the branches are similar to make it appear that they have been affected by the same environmental conditions.

–Branches in the back are shorter than those on the sides.

–No two branches are on the same level.

–No branches cross the front of the trunk.

–The trunk line is clearly visible from the front of the bonsai, with front-facing branches occurring only near the apex.

Suitable Plants Plant stock for this style must be fairly straight—or flexible enough to be wired straight—with a good number of branches to work on. The basic line is vertical, with the apex directly over the center of the trunk base. The apex may also bend slightly toward the front of the tree. The best plant material for this style includes evergreens and deciduous conifers.

Chinese podocarpus, formal upright, 39 inches tall

Informal Upright Style | *Moyogi*

This style is probably the most popular one in the bonsai world. It depicts a tree in nature that has suffered from the elements, with a trunk line showing contortion and branches that sag. In nature, this shape is created by the constant breaking of the trunk line by storms, ice, snow, or the actions of animals and insects. In creating this style, you can start with a tree that already shows the stresses that nature has imposed on it, or you may create the trunk movement by the use of wire and other methods.

Basic Design Rules

• The trunk line defines this style. It must show movement that appears natural. Choose the side of the trunk that best shows off the movement as the front of the tree.

• The trunk curves should be spaced closer together as you go up the trunk, which should taper from base to apex.

• The apex of the trunk should be directly over of the center of the trunk base.

• The roots should be spread out from all sides of the trunk horizontally. To support the movement of the trunk, the roots should be strongest to the left and right of the trunk. Avoid letting roots grow directly from the front of the trunk straight toward the viewer.

Willow-leaf fig, informal upright, 22 inches tall

- The first branch should be to the left or right of the trunk as viewed from the front of the tree. It is usually placed one-third of the way from the base of the tree and outside the first curve.

- Ideally, lateral branches should start at the outside of all curves. Back branches often grow from the midpoint between curves.

- Branches should never arise from the inside of a curve. There are two reasons for this: Artistically, a line from the inside of the curve will stop the eye as you look at the tree; and horticulturally, as the trunk grows, it will cut off the vascular tissue that feeds such a branch, eventually killing it.

- As in all bonsai, no branch should be placed directly over another branch. The shade caused by the upper branch will weaken the lower one.

- Each branch must be carefully positioned and shaped to indicate its age and health. The largest branches are typically found near the bottom of the tree, with progressively smaller and thinner branches approaching the apex.

- The basic rules of proportion described in the formal upright style should be followed with this style also.

Suitable Plants Most species of woody plants lend themselves to this very popular style, as long as the leaf size is in proportion with the design and the tree overall.

Slanting Style | *Shakan*

Looking at trees in nature, one often sees individuals that have been tilted to one side by the forces of wind or water, or ones that lean at an angle reaching for sunlight. These trees have developed strong root systems on one side to counter the weight of the tree's slant to the other side. As artists develop a bonsai in this style, they must carefully observe its counterparts in the real world to duplicate their shapes. For this design to work, balance must be achieved visually by size and placement of the roots and branches.

Basic Design Rules

- The trunk should rise at an angle between 30 and 75 degrees from the soil surface, with the apex above the bonsai container but never over the base of the tree.

- The line of the trunk may be straight (formal) or show motion (informal).

- To balance the tree, the root system should be heavier on the side that faces away from the slant.

Chinese podocarpus, slanting style, 38 inches tall

• The root system on the inside of the slant will often appear crushed, reflecting the effect of the lean.

• Branch placement and angle should help the tree in its balancing act. The lower branches may be longer in order to balance the tree against the force of gravity. When depicting a tree leaning or almost falling into a stream, there may be branches that stretch out over the stream toward the light. The angle of the branches will depend on the trunk's angle of slant and the vision of the artist.

• When positioning the bonsai in its container, balance remains an important consideration. The tree should be planted so that the slanting trunk reaches over the greater part of the container.

Suitable Plants Many woody plants can be used as long as the leaf size is in proportion with the design.

Semi-Cascade Style | *Han-kengai*

This style is meant to depict a tree hanging from the side of a cliff by the seashore or a stream. The tree grows over the edge of the pot, and the trunk bends downward beyond the rim of the container but not below its base.

Basic Design Rules

- The trunk line should grow out from the container at an angle and then bend downward. This angle should be as sharp as possible to aid in the illusion of the cascading tree.

- The larger the trunk base, the more stable the root system spread should appear. It should be more substantial on the side opposite the cascade.

- This style may have one or more trunk lines, one or two being the most common. When a second trunk line is used, it should form a small informal upright or slanting style reaching upward near the main bend or even somewhere farther down on the cascading trunk.

Chinese podocarpus, semi-cascade, 16 1/2 inches tall

- The branches also need to tell the story of the tree's growth. Their bend and placement should show where "nature" has affected the growth of the tree.

- The trick to keeping the lower cascading tip alive is to position the pot at a 45-degree angle early in the spring growing season, with the branches tipped up toward the sunlight. This will allow the branches to grow at the proper rate. After the initial growing season, the bonsai can be grown in its normal position.

Suitable Plants Many species work well, though it is probably easiest to start with a plant that is showing cascading or rambling growth or one that offers an abundance of pliable branches.

Full Cascade Style | *Kengai*

This bonsai style follows the rules of semi-cascade except that the cascading line falls below the base of the container. This requires that the bonsai be displayed on a stand so that the trunk line can extend as far as it needs to. Aesthetically, the tree must never touch the surface of the stand upon which it is displayed.

Suitable Plants Even though many tree species work well for cascade bonsai, try to envision the species growing as a cascade in nature. If it occurs in nature, then it will work in bonsai.

Asian jasmine, full cascade, 32 inches from the highest point to the lowest

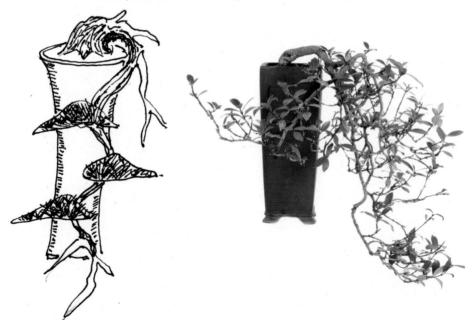

Other Styles

As you progress in bonsai, there are many other styles you can work with. Most of these follow the basic principles of the five basic styles. Once you have learned and practiced the basics, you can start exploring.

Broom Style

Broom-style bonsai resemble the old trees found along city streets or in orchards. A deciduous species is groomed to form a crown of radial branches that show a great deal of ramification (branching twigs), thereby creating a beautiful reflection of an old tree. Some broom styles have a main trunk line that extends from the base of the trunk to the apex; others have branches radiating from one central point, as shown in the drawing.

Weeping Style

In nature, weeping trees like willows are often found in damp areas and along streams and lakes. Bonsai artists replicate this vision by the careful use of wire to train a tree like a willow or weeping cherry. To create the form in miniature, wire each branch so that it bends upward, and then create a severe downward bend to style the weep.

Exposed Root Style

In nature, rain and weather can erode soil from the base of a tree, slowly exposing its roots over the years. Bonsai artists like to exaggerate this effect and show a great deal of root structure. This effect must be developed over a long period of time by baring only a bit of the roots each year and allowing the exposed area to harden off.

Root Over Rock Style

When a seed lands in a crack in a rock and finds enough soil to survive, the plant's roots may eventually grow to spread among the thin layers of soil and moss across the rock. In another scenario, the roots slowly grow over and around the rock to the soil below, partially encasing the rock. In bonsai, this effect is created by spreading roots over a rock and then allowing the roots to develop. One way to do this is to bury the rock among the roots when the plant is potted, and let them grow for a period of years before slowly exposing them over time and allowing them to harden off, as done with the exposed root style.

Double Trunk Style

This style depicts a tree with two trunks. The trunks, usually of two trees of different diameters, have grown together at the base, and the two trees are styled as one. No branches are permitted to grow between the trunks.

Raft Style

In the natural scenario this style seeks to emulate, a woodland tree is damaged by a storm and blown over, breaking the branches on the downward side. Over time, roots develop from the trunk resting on the soil, and the remaining branches (rising vertically from the undamaged side of the trunk) grow to look like new trees connected by the old trunk. In bonsai, a one-sided tree is wired and laid horizontally on soil, branchless side down. By nicking the bark to expose the cambium layer on the underside of the trunk and dusting it with rooting powder, the growth of roots is facilitated. A straight trunk usually forms a straight line of trees; using a curved trunk creates a more interesting pattern of trees that resembles a small grove.

Clump Style

When a cone or fruit containing several seeds falls in fertile soil and several trees grow at the same time, they may merge to form a tree with multiple trunks. Each trunk naturally bends outward from the group to reach for the light. The clump style in bonsai is created by planting a number of seedlings tightly together and styling them to form outward-reaching trunks.

Forest Style

Using five or more trees, artists can create bonsai resembling small or large forests. Sometimes the forest is styled to look as if it reaches far into the distance. By placing smaller trees in front and progressively larger ones behind, a far-view perspective can be achieved. Another perspective—that of a viewer amid the trees and looking at the forest stretching beyond—is created by placing larger plants in the front. In all cases, use trees of different diameters and heights and arrange them so that no three trees are placed in a straight line when viewed from the front or the side. The trees are all placed at different distances from each other. The overall effect is a canopy resembling a scalene triangle.

Literati Style

The literati style of bonsai is meant to show the essence of a tree. A literati has a beautiful, thin, and unique trunk line. Branches are kept to a minimum. This style is often thought to be the most difficult to achieve. Only a bonsai artist who has mastered all the rules and created great designs can successfully break the classic rules and create elegant literati.

Tip pruning, cutting new growth back to one or two sets of leaves, is probably the most time-consuming pruning task that will help keep your bonsai looking well groomed.

Pruning Primer

Robert Mahler

Regardless of a bonsai's age and species, regular pruning is essential for its life span. Shape is critical—balance is the aesthetic goal—and a healthy, attractive tree is the reward for good pruning. When you are just learning to shape bonsai, take some time to observe the structure of mature bonsai and familiarize yourself with the basic styling guidelines. Before reaching for the bonsai shears or knob cutters, remember that bonsai pruning accomplishes four essential tasks: It develops the shape of the tree; it encourages a dense, yet well-structured canopy; it keeps the tree small; and it maintains a balance between the tree's canopy and its root system. Through judicious pruning, the bonsai aboveground is kept to a size that the limited root system belowground can support.

Pruning Young Bonsai Begin developing your bonsai as early in the tree's life as possible. Initially, pruning should take precedence over showy displays of flowers or fruit, which consume a lot of a tree's energy and deplete its resources. Be ruthless and sacrifice immediate gratification for the long-term beauty and vitality of your tree.

Pruning to Preserve Flowers and Fruit Once a bonsai has achieved the shape you desire, time your pruning to preserve its flowers and the fruit developing from them. Over time you may learn to distinguish leaf buds from flower buds by shape, but it's not always easy. If you're not sure how to tell the two types of buds apart on a particular tree, refer to a tree manual. (Also note that some trees have beautiful flowers when they grow in the landscape but do not produce flowers when they are grown as bonsai.)

The Right Time to Prune Indoor bonsai are usually tropical, subtropical, or warm-temperate in origin, and season is usually not relevant to pruning. The best time for the job is when a tree is in active growth, and for these trees that could be at any moment, though it is probably safe to say that trees are most likely to grow most vigorously in late spring and summer, especially if they are spending the warmer months outside. Observe each tree closely and watch for new buds at the tips. Once buds have elongated and two or more new leaves are emerging, it's time to start thinking about pruning the new growth.

Containing Size and Promoting a Dense Canopy

Left unchecked, most trees grow most strongly at the tips. Proper pruning balances a bonsai's growth, redistributing vigor as evenly as possible across the entire canopy. To achieve this goal, cut back new growth so that just two, or at most four, leaves remain on each little branchlet. Provided that the buds—which sit directly below each leaf—are healthy, the result will be a new branchlet emerging at each bud. In essence, by pruning the tips, you are multiplying the tree's leaf buds by two, promoting good light exposure for each leaf, and in certain species, keeping leggy growth in check. Though it may sound drastic, the result is well worth the effort: a dense and well-defined, sculptured canopy.

Developing the Basic Style of a Bonsai

Together with wiring, pruning is the main way to shape a bonsai over time. Like virtually everything else in the world of bonsai, it is equal parts art and skill and requires plenty of patience and a good eye. Develop a pruning plan that stretches over several years, anticipating the tree's growth, and remove unwanted branches—over time. Keep the long-term health of the tree in mind as you style it: An undesirable branch left in place for a few years may actually benefit the tree as its leaves photosynthesize and nurture the tree and help it grow a strong, thick trunk.

- Remove branches that are too thick in comparison with the trunk, usually ones more than a third the circumference of the trunk.

- Remove branches that emerge at the wrong spot in relation to the balance of the tree.

- Cut back straight branches that are too thick to be guided with wire. See "Clip, Grow, and Wire" below for the option to cut the branch and let it redevelop with a more pleasing shape and diameter.

Molding the Shape of a Branch

The branches of your bonsai should look as if nature had determined their shape, each one showing graceful and plausible movement as well as taper. An arrow-straight branch is not part of the plan. To create movement and taper, bonsai artists rely on a technique called clip and grow, a start-and-stop method in which you allow a branch to grow, then cut it back part of the way, let it grow, cut it back part of the way, and so on. To do this, cut a branch back to a bud that points in the direction you want the branch to grow, allow the bud to expand and grow, then cut the new branch back, let it grow again, then cut again. At every cut, the branch changes direction, developing a dynamic shape that tapers beautifully.

Clip, Grow, and Wire When you've mastered this basic pruning concept, you can try to combine it with wiring. Cut a wayward or overly straight branch back to a favorable bud, then wire the remaining pliable branch section to gently guide its growth in the direction you want it. In some cases, this technique is an alternative to removing a problematic branch outright. (For tips on wiring technique, see "Wiring Basics," page 26.)

Pruning Branches to Open up the Canopy

When you open up the canopy of a mature tree, you are pruning for style and health at the same time, preserving or promoting growth that is essential and removing excess plant material. The need to remove branches from mature bonsai varies among species and from one tree to the next. Generally speaking, a super-fast-growing tree

A dwarf brush cherry before and after pruning. A well-defined, sculpted canopy with its growth evenly distributed over the entire tree is the result of judicious trimming.

A top view of a branch section of the dwarf brush cherry before pruning and then after—showing the open branching that allows light to reach all the leaves equally.

like the tropical serissa (*Serissa japonica*) will require much more aggressive pruning to manage its growth and keep its canopy beautiful than a slow-growing desert dweller like elephant tree (*Bursera fagaroides*). Know your tree's growth habit before you start, and let yourself be guided by visual cues, such as canopy density. A full canopy is, of course, one of the basic goals of bonsai pruning, but branches can easily become too dense to allow optimal light penetration or might grow in a way that clutters up the design or otherwise interferes with the tree's well-being and beauty. When that happens, it's time to open up the canopy.

- Remove branches that grow straight up or down.

- Remove one of two crossing branches or cut it back to a bud that points in a more favorable direction.

- Remove one of any two branches emerging exactly opposite each other. Which one to cut and which one to leave depends on the branches immediately above and below. Step back before each cut and check your tree's balance to avoid a lopsided look.

- If two branches emerge exactly above each other, one should go. Before you prune, though, check if one or both are pliable enough to guide with wire and be gently nudged apart for better light exposure and balance.

Once the branching is less dense, individual leaves receive more light, which promotes stronger growth and more leaf production, which in turn allows the tree to photosynthesize more and grow—and all that growth gives the bonsai artist more opportunities for guiding the tree's development.

Balancing Canopy and Roots

If you are repotting and root pruning a tree, you need to downsize the canopy to bring it back in balance with the reduced root system. For beginning bonsai growers it's advisable to remove foliage right after repotting. As a general rule, remove about the same percentage of leaves and roots. If you plan to work on shaping the tree, give it at least a month to recover from the serious intervention of repotting, root pruning, and foliage reduction. Observe your tree and shape it when it is once again showing signs of new growth. For most trees it is safe and recommended to trim off about half the new growth that develops each year.

Care After Pruning

- Be vigilant when you water a tree after you have pruned it. It will most likely need less water than before because it has fewer leaves to supply with water.

- If you are only pruning tips, you can place your tree back in its usual spot when you have finished working.

- When you prune out entire branches or branch sections to open up the canopy, it's best to keep the tree in a somewhat shadier position for a few days and then expose it slowly to brighter light conditions. The transition period allows leaves that were previously shaded by others time to adapt to the brighter light.

Do not try this on your landscape trees: To remove a branch on a tree planted in a bonsai pot, make a flush to slightly concave cut with knob cutters and seal the wound with cut paste.

Bonsai tools: wooden tweezers, wire cutters, metal tweezers, root hook, bonsai shears, brush, knob cutters, long-handled bonsai shears

BONSAI TOOLS AND GOOD SANITATION

Always use sharp cutting tools. They make clean cuts that close up properly. When you have finished pruning, use bonsai tweezers to clean up any debris or weeds that have collected in the interior of your tree or at its base. They may harbor fungi and other pathogens. Clean all your tools before you move from one tree to the next, to reduce the risk of spreading disease. Denatured alcohol, which can be found at your local hardware store, is a good choice for cleaning.

Bonsai shears, or bud scissors, as they are sometimes called, have extended blades that make them the ideal tool for tip pruning. Bonsai shears are also the right tool to trim branches up to one-half inch in diameter.

Knob cutters are the choice for branches over one-half inch in diameter. Always cut flush with the trunk when you remove entire branches. A clean cut promotes good callusing. (See photos, facing page.)

Cut Paste Cuts that are over one-half inch in diameter are usually sealed with cut paste. Apply a small amount of paste by hand to the cut area and smooth it to the edges. Replace the cut paste every four weeks. There are several brands of cut paste available; all are imported from Japan and can be purchased online. Lately there has been discussion on the effectiveness of cut paste, and you will see a variety of other products on the market. No matter what product you use, be sure to keep an eye on the wound, changing the covering regularly and watching for signs of rotting, disease, or pest infestation.

Together with pruning, wiring is the way to develop the shape and guide the growth of a bonsai. Watch the tree's growth and avoid letting the wire eat into the bark and cause damage, as above.

Wiring Basics

Robert Mahler

The fundamental reason to wire a bonsai is to adjust its shape, so the practice is mostly concerned with aesthetics rather than the health of the tree. If the thought of deftly coiling a strand of wire around a delicate branch or the precious trunk of a prized tree makes you blanch, rest assured that this is a learnable skill. What follows is an overview of materials, techniques, and tricks to help you get started.

Aluminum or Copper Wire Beginners typically start with aluminum because it's more malleable than copper, it's reusable, and it's less expensive. Copper has its merits—it's stronger and offers superior holding power. However, some species are allergic to it, so should you decide to use copper, be sure to do your homework.

Wire Length and Gauge Always start with a wire that is one and a half times the length of the branch you're targeting. The gauge of the wire is also important. For example, thicker wire provides a stronger hold than smaller-gauge wire, which makes it more appropriate for larger branches. A good rule of thumb is to use wire that is approximately one-third the diameter of the branch you want to wrap.

Wiring Practice First and foremost, patience and caution are essential to avoid damage to your specimen. Before you apply wires to a living tree, go out to your garden and harvest some twigs of different diameters and pliability and practice your wire-wrapping technique. Familiarize yourself with the placement of wires on existing bonsai and observe the spacing and tension. When you feel comfortable with your level of expertise, move on to live bonsai.

Wiring Two Branches Placing your first wire can be intimidating. A common error among beginners is to wire branches individually. For the wiring to be effective, you need to wrap two branches with a single wire (this is called anchoring). The tension between the branches will act as a support and hold each in its desired position. Over time, the repositioned branch or branches will adjust their growth pattern to the desired configuration.

Wiring Trunk and Branches If you don't have a suitable second branch available for anchorage, work your wire up the trunk from the soil. In this case, the trunk works as a stabilizer. Regardless of which route you take, always start the process from the bottom up and from the inside out. Should you decide to wire the trunk in addition to two branches, start with the trunk.

Wire Placement Wiring should always be kept neat, and wires should not crisscross. Place the wire on the branch or trunk at a 45-degree angle. Coil the wire firmly around the branch or trunk in even loops. As you work the wire up the branch or trunk, hold the latest coil in place so as not to strangle the tree as you continue on your way up and outward. Check your handiwork along the way: If the spacing is uneven or if the wire itself is coiled too loosely, it cannot adequately hold the branch in place.

Wrapping two branches with one wire lets you move one into position while the other anchors it.

Applying and Removing Wires Generally speaking, the wiring of a tree is done all at once, not on a branch now and then. The removal of wire is also done all at one time and is critical to the well-being of your tree. Use wire cutters to remove thick wires; if the wire is thin and easily pliable, carefully uncoil it the same way it was applied.

Vigilance and Timing On average, wires stay on a tree for six months to a year. But keep an eye on them, as every tree responds to them differently. If you notice that a wire is eating into a branch, remove it immediately. Wiring does cause stress to the tree, so should you wish to rewire, give the tree time to recuperate first. A year should suffice.

When to Wire a Bonsai Whether you start with a seedling, cutting, air layer, or nursery plant, the shape of your bonsai in the making is usually achieved with a combination of well-executed pruning and the occasional deployment of wires. Work on seedlings, cuttings, or small air layers when the plants show signs of new growth and fresh foliage is emerging. Limit your efforts to healthy plants that show no evidence of disease or insect infestation. With a seedling, a good rule of thumb is to begin the wiring process approximately two years after germination. With cuttings, start the wiring process as young as possible, typically when the tree is anywhere from a year to two years of age. Since seedlings and cuttings can require quite a bit of waiting, it's sensible to

Start with a wire that's one and a half times the length and approximately one-third the diameter of the branch or trunk section.

When shaping a tree, all needed wires are usually applied at the same time. They stay on for six months to a year, depending on how easily the tree holds its new position.

work with several specimens from the start. A bit of planning will afford you a small collection of young trees and multiple opportunities to hone your wiring skills.

With an air layer, or rooted branch, the average start time is within two to three years after it has been potted. Air layers are typically chosen for their inherent design features and usually have a desirable bonsai-like shape from the onset, so wiring should be less exacting.

If you begin with nursery stock, look for a specimen whose trunk has good natural curvature. The alternative would be a specimen with a trunk that is thin and flexible enough to be wired into a desired shape.

Encyclopedia of Bonsai for Indoors

Robert Mahler and Julian Velasco

On the following pages you will encounter 24 handsome trees suited to indoor bonsai culture. With a few notable exceptions, the species are tropical, subtropical, or Mediterranean in origin, which primes them for adapting to the growing conditions found inside the average home. Trees were selected for inherent bonsai qualities like short internodes and amenability to pot culture, with a view to providing a mixture of deciduous and evergreen species suitable for training in different sizes in a variety of styles. Within these parameters, selected bonsai offer a range of leaf sizes, textures, and shapes as well as lots of bark choices, from smooth to rough to scaly or peeling. Quite a few of the trees feature beautiful flowers followed by attractive fruits one or even several times a year. Bear in mind that flowers and then fruit are usually found on mature specimens. Most often, especially when they are very large and showy, flowers are removed from young trees to redirect their energy toward vegetative growth—specifically the development of a strong trunk and beautiful branches. Other trees may flower when they grow in the landscape but rarely do so in bonsai culture.

Each portrait highlights the tree's best bonsai attributes and features a section on growing that outlines basic care requirements for light, temperature, watering, and repotting. There is also a section on styling, with tips for pruning and wiring. As you browse through the encyclopedia and choose your bonsai, look for plants that favor the growing conditions you can provide in the microclimate of your home. Refer to the other chapters in this book for a more in-depth look at bonsai care, health, and styles.

This European olive, trained as an informal upright, is about 24 inches tall and more than a hundred years old. The bonsai was developed from a gnarly trunk found growing in the wild.

Bougainvillea Species and Cultivars
Bougainvillea

Because it develops a large trunk and grows rapidly under proper conditions, bougainvillea makes an excellent medium to large bonsai. It has sharp thorns and dark, glossy heart-shaped leaves that end with a drip tip, a pointy end that allows the leaf to shed water efficiently. The flowers come in a variety of colors: yellow, purple, pink, orange, red, and white. The blooms—three papery bracts surrounding small tubular flowers—are abundant and fragrance-free. There are a lot of variegated cultivars with leaves that are typically a mixture of yellow and green, but they are generally less robust than species or green-leafed cultivars and are not traditionally used for bonsai in Japan. The species are native to the rainforests of South America.

Growing

Light Bright western or southern window exposure is ideal. If that's not available, grow-lights are mandatory. Bougainvillea may drop its leaves in winter if there's not enough light.

Temperature Range This plant prefers warm climates, ideally around 65°F to 75°F; it can tolerate cooler temperatures but will drop its leaves and go dormant. Move the tree outdoors in summer, but be sure to return it inside as soon as temperatures drop to 65°F.

Watering Keep bougainvillea evenly moist. Reduce watering if the plant goes dormant. To induce flowering in summer, allow the specimen to dry out and wilt for three to four hours, then begin watering normally. Expect flower production to begin one to two weeks after wilting. Fertilize weekly with a well-balanced fertilizer at half strength. Reduce to once every two to three weeks in winter. Bougainvillea likes acidic soil, so supplement with an acidic fertilizer for azaleas or camellias at half strength once a month.

Bougainvillea × *buttiana* 'Raspberry Ice', semi-cascade, about 10 inches tall and 16 inches wide

Repotting Bougainvillea likes to be root-bound and should be repotted every two to three years. It does not develop a strong fibrous root ball until the plant is quite old. Remove circling roots and extra-long woody roots, leaving shorter woody roots, which are needed to stabilize the tree. Keep as much of the fibrous roots as possible.

Recommended Soil Blend A good blend is 50 percent Metro mix 510 and 50 percent lava rock.

Getting Started The species is propagated from seeds, cuttings, air layers, or nursery stock.

Styling

Pruning Bougainvillea needs pruning only when the specimen is actively growing. The plant does get leggy easily and can be pruned back hard to preserve its shape. For flowering and design purposes, let each branch grow out to four or five sets of leaves and then prune back to two sets of leaves. Flowers only occur on new growth and should be removed on young plants to preserve their resources.

Wiring Branches are brittle in general and easy to break, so wire with caution. Use aluminum wire only.

Recommended Styles Informal upright, cascade, literati, twin trunk, and forest style are good choices. —*R.M.*

Bucida molinetii | Black Olive

Black olive lends itself naturally to bonsai, in part because of its tight growth habit and short, thin branches that quite dramatically change direction at the nodes. The small leaves are dark blue-green in color and closely spaced. The black olive tolerates salt quite well, so it's an excellent choice for bonsai enthusiasts near the sea who plan to summer collections outdoors. Flowers are cream; the fruit starts out green and develops into a reddish brown. This small tree grows 10 to 20 feet tall, is native to southern Florida, and was formerly known as *Bucida spinosa*.

Specimen above: Informal upright, 12 inches tall, about 20 years old and in training for 10 years

Growing

Light Bright light is necessary indoors and outdoors.

Temperature Range A range between 65°F and 75°F is recommended. Move the tree outside for the summer, and return it indoors when nighttime temperatures drop to 50°F to 55°F in fall.

Watering Water frequently, but allow the soil to dry slightly between each watering. Fertilize weekly with a balanced fertilizer at half strength. Reduce to once every two to three weeks in winter.

Repotting Repot annually in late winter. Prune the roots minimally, about half an inch all around the edges of the root ball.

Recommended Soil Blend This tree prefers alkaline soil: 25 percent Metro mix 510, and 75 percent lava rock.

Getting Started Cuttings, air layers, or nursery stock are recommended. Growing from seed can be discouraging due to their low germination rate.

Styling

Pruning When new growth emerges and four to five sets of new leaves are present, you can safely prune. Be sure to remove excess branches to allow good light penetration, but be careful of the thorns, which can be 1½ inches long. Cut them off as needed, or wet the tree about half an hour before you want to prune to soften them slightly.

Wiring Branches on this species are notably flexible, another advantage for beginners. Wire the main branches and trunk at an early age.

Recommended Styles The species' tight growth habit offers lots of options, making this a great tree to experiment styling with, particularly for the informal upright, cascade, and windswept styles. *—R.M.*

Bursera fagaroides | Elephant Tree

Also known as fragrant bursera, this succulent shrub or small tree lends itself perfectly to *chuhin* (midsize bonsai). Elephant tree has a beautiful light brown stocky, swollen trunk with an attractive flaky bark that gives a feeling of age early on. The small blue-green leaves are handsome, and the tree surprises the attentive viewer with small light blue to gray berries tucked tightly near their bases. The fruit is more easily seen in the colder months, when the tree drops its leaves; the seasonal lack of foliage also emphasizes the tree's sculptural qualities. This desert plant is native from northwestern Mexico to southern Arizona, where it thrives in hot daytime and considerably cooler nighttime temperatures, growing to 16 feet.

Growing

Light Bright light is essential. While the tree is indoors, if western or southern exposure is not available, grow-lights are highly recommended.

Temperature Range The ideal temperature for spring and summer is 70°F to 85°F. For maximum growth, place the tree outdoors in summer. Temperatures should drop to 55°F to 60°F during fall and winter. This will allow the tree to develop bronze to yellow leaf color in fall and transition into a beautiful defoliated state in winter.

Watering Allow the soil to almost dry out between waterings. During winter keep the soil almost dry. When the tree is actively growing, fertilize weekly or biweekly with a well-balanced fertilizer at half strength. In fall and winter, reduce fertilizing to every three weeks if temperatures are kept above 55°F. Stop fertilizing when the tree goes dormant.

Repotting Because its roots will not fill the pot very quickly, the tree should be fine if it is repotted every five to eight years. When repotting becomes necessary, summer is the best time to do it.

Specimen above: slanting style, 20 inches tall

Recommended Soil Blend A very fast draining soil is important to prevent overwatering and root rot. Use little or no organic material in the mix in order to slow breakdown of the soil, which needs to stay viable for quite a long time.

Getting Started Propagate the species from seeds or cuttings.

Styling

Pruning Elephant tree responds well to clip-and-grow directional pruning. Let the branches grow for a bit, and cut them when the tree is in an active growth phase. It is not necessary to cut back or pinch the tender new leaves; the plant grows short lateral stems from the main branches, which lend themselves to a natural look without much help from the bonsai artist.

Wiring The branches of this tree are very brittle, so be very cautious when you attempt wiring—just add some gentle movement where appropriate.

Recommended Styles Slant, windswept, and informal upright are appropriate styles for fragrant bursera. —*J.V.*

Buxus microphylla var. *japonica*
Japanese Boxwood

This evergreen shrub is excellent for both large and small bonsai because of its small, tight growth and its ability to thrive in a container. Leaves are light green, rounded, and dense. Japanese boxwood does occasionally flower, but it's rare. Flowers are small, inconspicuous, and yellow in color. It is one of the few temperate cold-hardy plants that do well as indoor bonsai, possibly because it is adaptable to a wide range of growing conditions outdoors.

Specimen above: multitrunk slant, 9 inches tall

Growing

Light Southern or western sun exposure is recommended; otherwise provide grow-lights.

Temperature Range Boxwood prefers cool winters (inside), approximately 55°F to 65°F. For the rest of the year, 65°F to 75°F is a good average. Although this is a temperate shrub, it does quite well in cool indoor conditions. It benefits from a summer spent outdoors, but move it back inside when temperatures drop to 50°F.

Watering Keep this plant evenly moist, and don't let it dry out. Fertilize weekly with a well-balanced fertilizer at half strength; reduce to once every two to three weeks in winter. Supplement with an acidic fertilizer for azaleas or camellias at half strength once a month.

Repotting Repot every other year.

Recommended Soil Blend Use 50 percent Metro mix 510, 25 percent lava rock, and 25 percent Turface.

Getting Started Use cuttings, air layers, and nursery stock.

Styling

Pruning Developing the boxwood's basic shape is all about decision making. Budding is prolific, and there are lots of branches to choose from when styling. The species can also be cut back hard in early spring and then developed with the clip-and-grow method. Once the tree's shape is set, let the branchlets grow four to five sets of leaves, and then cut back to two sets of leaves for a well-defined, sculpted profile.

Wiring Japanese boxwood branches are extremely brittle and break easily, so take great caution when wiring. It may be easier to look for a plant with good trunk curvature and branches emerging at the desired spots to begin with, and then focus on pruning.

Recommended Styles Informal upright and clump-style bonsai styles work nicely with boxwood. —*R.M.*

Calliandra surinamensis
Surinam Powder-Puff

This South American native makes for a great small to medium bonsai because of its dense foliage, abundant branches, and speedy growth. It also takes readily to pot culture. Leaves are dark green, pinnate, oblong and evergreen. They close up at night and reopen in the morning. The name-giving pink powder-puff flowers peek through the dark foliage. The fragrant puffs, one of the main attractions that make this low-branching shrub a popular garden choice in warm climates, are usually sparser and paler on bonsai. The shrub grows to 15 feet wide and tall.

Growing

Light Bright light is required—a southern or western exposure is best; use grow-lights if not available.

Temperature Range This plant prefers cool winters (inside), at approximately 55°F to 65°F. It will be happy summering outdoors, with temperatures around 70°F to 85°F, for the rest of the year.

Watering Keep the soil evenly moist, and don't allow it to dry out between watering. Fertilize weekly with a balanced fertilizer at half strength; reduce to once every two to three weeks in winter. Supplement this regimen with an acidic fertilizer formulated for azaleas or camellias at half strength once a month.

Repotting Repot every two years while the tree is in active growth and the weather is nice and warm. You can safely remove up to about a third of the fibrous roots.

Recommended Soil Blend This species prefers rich, well-drained acidic soil: Try 50 percent Metro mix 510, 25 percent lava rock, and 25 percent Turface.

Getting Started It's recommended to start with nursery stock, air layers, or cuttings.

Specimen above: informal upright, 20 inches tall, trained from a stump collected in 1995

Styling

Pruning Prune during the growing season, cutting new branchlets back to two sets of leaves once new growth has developed at least four or five sets of leaves. This species has a tendency to develop spindly branches: Cut each back to a bud that points in a favorable direction and let it regrow, then cut back again (the clip-and-grow method) to achieve strong, beautifully articulated branches over time.

Wiring This species is quite resilient, and wiring may be done at any time during the year. Concentrate on younger branches that have just turned woody. Older branches are quite brittle.

Recommended Styles Try styling Surinam powder-puff in the informal upright or formal upright bonsai forms. —R.M.

Callistemon linearis
Narrow-Leafed Bottlebrush

If you like flashy flowers, this plant is for you. In late winter you'll be delighted with a display of long cylinders of bright red clustered flowers. The many delicate flower puffs of each "brush" contrast with the small, narrow foliage. The show can last for more than a month, but that's not all the tree has to offer—the fissured, corky light brown bark easily gives the impression of an ancient tree, and the fine foliage is evergreen. The leaf size is in scale for small trees, but the large showy flowers dangling from the ends of the branches look more proportionate in a mid- to large-size bonsai. In nature, the Australian native grows about 10 feet high and 15 feet wide. It is adapted to hot and dry environments, which primes it for conditions indoors.

Specimen above: informal upright, 37 inches tall

Growing

Light The more light the bonsai receives, the tighter the growth. A western or southern window exposure is good, otherwise supplement with artificial lights. This tree benefits from a summer spent outdoors.

Temperature Range Ideal temperatures are about 75°F to 90°F in spring and summer and 55°F to 65°F in fall and winter.

Watering Don't let the soil get bone dry, but let it dry out somewhat between waterings to keep the soil and bonsai healthy. During hot summer weather, increase watering, but never let the soil remain soggy. Fertilize weekly with a well-balanced fertilizer at half strength during active growth. In fall and winter, fertilize every two to three weeks as long as temperatures are above 55°F.

Repotting Repot every two to three years during late spring or early summer.

Recommended Soil Blend This tree prefers fast-draining bonsai soil.

Getting Started Propagate the species from seed or cuttings.

Styling

Pruning While the tree is young and in its developing phase, prune it back hard to achieve a basic structure and disregard the flowers. After the structure is set, allow the branches to grow, then cut them back while the tree is in active growth to encourage the tree to fill out. Keeping up with your pruning is very important because the tree has a tendency for legginess. Thin growth by removing branchlets that are growing straight up or down, but keep laterally growing shoots. Stop pruning a mature specimen by the end of summer—the flowers develop from end-of-season growth. Resume pruning after the tree finishes flowering.

Wiring As with most bonsai, it's best to wire pliable young growth. Older branches up to one-half inch in diameter can be wired and gently bent. As these are much less flexible than younger growth, they must be handled with care.

Recommended Styles Narrow-leafed bottlebrush can easily be styled in formal, informal, and slant styles. —*J.V.*

Camellia sasanqua
Fall-Blooming Camellia

This medium-size evergreen shrub native to Japan has an upright, fairly compact habit and inch-long leathery evergreen leaves. It makes for a nice small- to medium-size bonsai. Depending on the cultivar, of which there are many, the showy flowers come in a range of reds and pinks as well as white and bear no fragrance. Aptly named, this really is a fall-blooming camellia and will not bloom in spring, as many other camellias do.

Growing

Light This plant prefers southern or western exposure with bright full sun. If not available, use grow-lights. Camellias do well summering outdoors.

Temperature Range This camellia prefers cool winters (inside), with temperatures of approximately 55°F to 65°F. For the rest of the year, 65°F to 75°F is a good average. Move the plant back inside when temperatures drop to the 50s. This plant can tolerate a light frost, but the transition to indoor conditions is easier if the tree comes in beforehand; otherwise it may drop its flower buds.

Watering This plant needs a lot of water and prefers moist, acidic soil. Fertilize weekly with a balanced fertil-izer at half strength; reduce to once every two to three weeks in winter. Supplement with an acidic fertilizer for camellias at half strength once a month.

Repotting Repot annually in early spring. Cut back roots gently, removing no more than ten percent of the very fine feeder roots.

Recommended Soil Blend Camellias do well in 50 percent Metro mix 510, 25 percent lava rock, and 25 percent Turface.

Getting Started Nursery stock, cuttings, or air layers are recommended. Avoid nursery plants with trunks that are larger than a half inch in diameter unless they show good curvature and will not need wiring.

Specimen above: forest style, 25 inches tall and 30 inches wide

Styling

Pruning Gently prune mature camellias after flowering. On young specimens, let new growth develop up to four sets of leaves in spring, then cut back branchlets, leaving two sets of leaves with viable buds at the base. Camellias do not like to be pruned hard and will not sprout new growth from buds that sit farther back on mature, or woody, branches.

Wiring The fall-blooming camellia tends to grow straight and upright, and it has excessively brittle branches. To develop a pleasing shape, wiring the tree when it is very young or wiring a cutting, which is pliable, is likely to get the best results. Watch the tree closely and apply wires when the branches have become woody but before they turn brittle.

Recommended Styles Cascade, informal upright, and forest styles all work nicely. —*R.M.*

Carissa macrocarpa | Natal Plum

The Natal plum is a good choice for beginners since it's easy to grow and not particularly fussy. It is drought resistant and likes high humidity levels. The generally evergreen leaves are small, rounded with a tip, and dark green in color. This shrub produces fragrant white flowers that are followed by a purple plumlike fruit that's popular eaten raw or made into preserves in South Africa, where the plant is native. Natal plum also has sharp thorns up to half an inch long, which may be one way to explain its popularity as a hedge plant. This fast-growing shrub to small tree is commonly grown as an ornamental in southern gardens; it was formerly known as *Carissa grandiflora*.

Specimen above: cascade, 20 inches from highest point to lowest

Growing

Light Natal plum prefers at least four hours of direct sunlight a day; if growing indoors, keep it in a southern or western window or supplement with grow-lights.

Temperature Range A cool winter (inside) is preferred, approximately 60°F to 65°F. For the rest of the year, 70°F to 85°F is a good average. Summer Natal plum outdoors, and move it back inside when temperatures drop to 50°F to 55°F. If it gets too cold, Natal plum may drop its leaves.

Watering Water frequently, but let the soil dry slightly between watering to avoid root rot. Apply a balanced fertilizer at half strength weekly. Reduce applications to once every two to three weeks in winter.

Repotting Repot in early summer every other year.

Recommended Soil Blend Natal plum prefers sandy alkaline soil: 50 percent Metro mix 510, 25 percent turkey grit, and 25 percent Turface works well.

Getting Started Nursery stock, cuttings or air layers are recommended.

Styling

Pruning Anytime when the plant is in active growth, it may be pruned. Be careful of the thorns. Natal plum may become a bit leggy, but it can be pruned back hard when needed—it will grow back well. Blooms appear on new growth in midsummer to late summer. Remove budding flowers on young specimens—they sap the tree of energy and only appear at the tips of very leggy growth. Enjoy them when the tree has reached maturity and will produce flowers on much shorter growth.

Wiring This shrub's branches are flexible, so wiring should be simple. Even moderately large trunks, up to about three-fourths inch in diameter, can be wired and bent into the desired shape.

Recommended Styles Cascade and informal upright bonsai styles are recommended for this tree. —*R.M.*

Ebenopsis ebano | Texas Ebony

Because it grows rather slowly, North American native Texas ebony lends itself to small (*shohin*) or midsize (*chuhin*) bonsai. At night and in the early morning, bonsai enthusiasts are treated to the calming look of the evergreen leaflets neatly folded up along the central leaf stalk—a sight that never ceases to delight. Beware of the spines camouflaged beneath the foliage. The species grows in lowland areas from Texas south to Mexico and can reach an impressive 25 to 30 feet tall. Outdoors it produces lovely plumelike flower spikes and persistent woody seedpods, but these rarely form indoors. The tree thrives in hot, dry environments and has adapted to drop its leaves in times of drought and grow them back when water is again available. This species was formerly known as *Pithecellobium flexicaule*.

Growing

Light Western or southern window exposure is fine. The more light the tree gets, the better it will grow.

Temperature Range Texas ebony thrives in home temperatures of 70°F to 80°F. If temperatures remain in this range, the bonsai will not need a dormant or rest period. The tree can tolerate it down to the 30s, but exposed for a long period of time, the tree will react by dropping its leaves—which will grow back when temperatures become consistently warmer.

Watering Keep the soil slightly moist, allowing it to almost dry out before watering again. Wet soil conditions will cause root rot and yellowing leaves or even leaf drop; in severe cases death to entire branches or worse can occur. During active growth, fertilize weekly with a well-balanced fertilizer at half strength. In fall and winter, fertilize once every two to three weeks as long as temperatures are kept above 55°F.

Repotting Repot every three to four years in late spring or early summer.

Recommended Soil Blend Average fast-draining bonsai soil is preferred.

Specimen above: informal upright, 12 inches tall

Getting Started Propagate the species from seeds or cuttings. Soak seeds in water for 24 hours before planting.

Styling

Pruning To create graceful lines, clip new growth back to a set of leaves on each branchlet facing in the direction new branches are desired. Wiring is recommended in the initial stages of development, but the clip-and-grow method is best for shaping mature specimens because the tree's branches tend to grow in a zigzag pattern. With creative prun-

ing it's possible to form a very natural-looking tree. The typically small leaves make pinching unnecessary.

Wiring Start wiring when the twigs are still soft, and be careful to work around the spines or clip them off. Once branches harden off they are much more difficult to bend to shape.

Recommended Styles Most styles work for Texas ebony. Cascading styles are the most difficult because of the tree's rather hard wood. —J.V.

Ficus species | Figs

Fig trees are among the most popular plants trained for indoor bonsai. One reason is that many *Ficus* species can grow well in the lower light conditions available indoors. In addition, because of the incredible number of mostly tropical and subtropical species available, one can find many leaf sizes, shapes, and textures, along with different growth habits, to fit any bonsai size and style. Some species, like huge Indian banyan (*Ficus benghalensis*), have the ability to grow beautiful aerial roots from the trunk and branches. In the landscape, the canopy of this species can grow more than a hundred feet wide. Others are small shrubs, like mistletoe fig (*F. deltoidea*; see foliage and fruit on facing page, far right), or vines, like climbing fig (*F. pumila*).

Specimen above: willow-leaf fig, informal upright, 22 inches tall

Growing

Growing and styling tips focus on Chinese banyan (*Ficus microcarpa*) and willow-leaf fig (*F. cordata* subsp. *salicifolia*, leaf detail below, left), but most figs can be treated in the manner described here.

Light Figs do best in full sun but can adapt to lower light. A west-facing window would be fine.

Temperature Range Grow at warm temperatures—70°F to 85°F—all year. Figs do not need a dormant period. Summer the trees outdoors.

Watering Let the soil dry out somewhat between watering, but keep it just slightly moist. Raising the humidity with a humidity tray can help in the formation of aerial roots if desired. Fertilize weekly with a balanced fertilizer at half strength during spring and summer; in fall and winter, fertilize once every two to three weeks as growth slows.

Repotting Repotting should be done every one to two years in late spring or early summer. Figs handle root pruning with no problem.

Recommended Soil Blend Pot into a fast-draining bonsai soil.

Getting Started The species can usually be propagated from cuttings.

Styling

Both Chinese banyan and willow-leaf fig are fast growers. The main difference between the two is leaf size and shape. Chinese banyan has dark green oval leaves that tend to be a little larger and thicker than the narrow, pointed, lighter green leaves of willow-leaf fig.

Pruning Begin pruning in spring. Allow shoots to grow six to eight leaves, then prune back to two or three leaves. Because of the strong growth habit of figs, branching is quickly achieved once a trunk is developed. This is a plus for branch development, but it may cause upper branches to thicken too much, making them look out of scale. Keep up with pruning, and every few years when branches have thickened too much, prune them back to a thinner side branch and wire it into position, creating nice smooth taper over time.

Wiring Wire branches for movement while they are flexible. The aerial roots can be directed by guiding them with wire or inserting them into drinking straws split open vertically.

Recommended Styles Figs can be styled into any bonsai style. Root over rock, exposed root, and aerial root (banyan) styles are easy to achieve. —*J.V.*

Fortunella hindsii | Kumquat

This shrub or small tree makes for a fun bonsai, in part because of its bright orange fruits. They resemble miniature tangerines, are about the size of large peas, and start to form when the tree is just two to three years old. Kumquat develops into a respectable bonsai within five to ten years of seed germination, as the approximately seven-year-old seed-grown specimen on the facing page demonstrates. Flowers are tiny and white and bloom from September to October amid dark green oval leaves. The bark on a mature tree is tan and white and appears striped. Like many of its citrus family cousins, kumquat has thorns, but quite unlike most of the rest of the family, it comes true from seed. This plant is native to East Asia and generally grows to about 15 feet high.

Growing

Light Southern or western exposure is recommended; use grow-lights if adequate natural light is not available.

Temperature Range Kumquat prefers cool winters inside, at approximately 55°F to 65°F; 70°F to 85°F is a good average for the rest of the year. Summer the tree outside and move it back in when nighttime temperatures drop to the mid-50s. Even though the tree is quite cold tolerant, the transition to indoor conditions is less stressful when it happens at that time.

Watering Keep evenly moist during the growing season, and for the remainder of the year, let the soil dry between watering. Fertilize weekly with a balanced fertilizer at half strength. Reduce to once every two to three weeks in winter. Supplement with an acidic fertilizer for azaleas or camellias at half strength once a month.

Repotting Repot every two to three years. Kumquat tolerates root pruning well. It is okay to remove up to one third of the hair roots at one time.

Recommended Soil Blend A good combination is 50 percent Metro mix

Specimen above: semi-cascade, 6 inches tall

510, 25 percent lava rock, and 25 percent Turface.

Getting Started Buying nursery stock is the simplest way to start a kumquat bonsai; however, this species will grow true from seed—it's the only way to propagate besides grafting.

Styling

Pruning Be diligent about tip-pruning kumquat, and cut back new growth to two sets of leaves frequently. Avoid pruning it back hard, however. That will make it respond with leggy growth. It's not necessary to remove the flowers from young specimens; they and the fruits that develop from them are so small that they don't sap much energy from the tree. Enjoy them for a while and take them off once they start to get overripe or shrivel up.

Wiring Once they become slightly woody, wire the branches. It's okay to wire kumquats at any time of the year, just be mindful of the thorns.

Recommended Styles Informal upright and cascade styles both work nicely with kumquat. —*R.M.*

Gardenia jasminoides | Gardenia

Its arching habit makes this gardenia an excellent small to medium bonsai and naturally lends itself to the cascade style. Its evergreen leaves are bright to dark green and glossy, and the large, creamy-white waxy flowers bloom in winter and emit an intoxicating fragrance. The blooms are followed by a yellow-orange edible fruit. Native to China, the shrub grows to six feet tall and wide.

Specimen above: slanting style, 5 $1/2$ inches tall and 9 $1/2$ inches wide, about 40 years old and 35 years in training

Growing

Light Bright sun is preferred, with a southern or western window exposure indoors, or grow-lights if adequate natural light is unavailable.

Temperature Range Gardenia prefers cool winters (inside), approximately 55°F to 65°F; 70°F to 85°F is a good average for the rest of the year. Summer it outdoors and return inside when temperatures drop to the 50s.

Watering Keep the soil evenly moist during the growing season. In winter, let the soil dry out between watering. Fertilize weekly with a well-balanced fertilizer at half strength. Reduce to once every two to three weeks in winter. Supplement once a month with a fertilizer for acid lovers like azaleas and camellias.

Repotting Repot every other year in early spring. Remove no more than ten percent of the fibrous roots.

Recommended Soil Blend This species likes acidic soil. Try using 50 percent Metro mix 510, 25 percent lava rock, and 25 percent Turface.

Getting Started Nursery stock, air layers, and softwood cuttings are recommended for beginners.

Styling

Pruning Training the plant as a cascade takes advantage of its natural tendency to sprawl a bit. To develop a cascade, cut the branches back to encourage the development of dense branching and then wire them. To develop an informal upright, stake the plant until the trunk becomes woody enough to support itself. This may take several years. Prune young plants in spring once branchlets have developed four to six pairs of leaves, cutting back to two. Prune mature plants lightly after flowering ends.

Wiring This plant is easy to manipulate with wire and it can be done at any time. Once the plant has sprouted lots of growth, guide it with aluminum wire to achieve a pleasing shape. Be careful not to injure the bark, which is quite vulnerable.

Recommended Styles This plant's habit is conducive to both informal upright and cascade styles. —*R.M.*

Grewia occidentalis
Lavender Star Flower

This evergreen shrub is an excellent choice for small bonsai. It has small, tapering, shiny dark green leaves, and about three times a year, starlike mauve to purple flowers appear. The blooms are especially abundant from October through January and in early spring. On occasion, they are followed by berrylike fruits that hang in sets of four. These are dark brown at first and turn to reddish brown as they mature. This native of Africa is vigorous and fast growing. It's also quite drought tolerant, making it a good bonsai plant for beginners.

Growing

Light Lavender star flower prefers bright sun—try a western or southern window exposure. If not available, use grow-lights.

Temperature Range A good average temperature for this species is 65°F to 70°F. Summer it outdoors, returning it indoors when nighttime temperatures drop to the 50s.

Watering Keep the soil evenly moist. Fertilize weekly with a well-balanced fertilizer at half strength, and reduce it to once every two to three weeks in winter. Supplement occasionally with a fertilizer for acid lovers like azaleas and camellias. This species becomes chlorotic easily; it's a good idea to supplement with chelated iron once a year to avoid problems.

Repotting Repot every two years. The plant tolerates root pruning well. You can safely remove up to a third of the fine hair roots.

Recommended Soil Blend Pot this plant in 50 percent Metro mix 510, 25 percent lava rock, and 25 percent Turface.

Getting Started Nursery stock, cuttings, and air layers are recommended for beginners.

Specimen above: informal upright, about 30 inches tall

Styling

Pruning Lavender star flower is a vigorous grower. Prune the tips of this species back to two sets of leaves at any time of the year when the shoots have elongated. Remove the flowers from young trees to preserve the tree's energy as its shape is being developed. Prune mature specimens right after the blooms have dropped to maintain the form.

Wiring This shrub can be wired at any time of the year. It is easy to work with, but use aluminum wire only.

Recommended Styles Informal upright and cascade are good styling choices. —R.M.

Hedera helix | English Ivy

This evergreen vine native from Europe and northern Africa is very hardy
and has adapted to thrive in a very wide range of climatic conditions. It
is quite forgiving, easy to work with, and a good choice for beginners.
The vine produces shiny, waxy dark green leaves with palmate veins. The
small flowers are usually yellow-green and result in black berries in fall.
Even though it's a vine, it does develop a good woody trunk and is a great
choice for small to medium bonsai. There are lots of cultivars of English ivy,
including ones with yellow or white variegation—be sure to choose one with
small leaves.

Specimen above: multitrunk upright, 5 inches tall

Growing

Light English ivy prefers bright light; a window with southern or western exposure is good.

Temperature Range A good average for most of the year is 70°F to 85°F. Cool winters (inside), at approximately 55°F to 65°F, are ideal. English ivy benefits from a summer spent outdoors. Move it back inside in fall.

Watering Keep the soil evenly moist. Fertilize it with an acidic fertilizer for camellias every two weeks at half strength during the growing season. Stop fertilizer applications during winter.

Repotting Repot every two years. English ivy takes well to root pruning.

Recommended Soil Blend English ivy likes slightly acidic soil. Use 50 percent Metro mix 510, 25 percent lava rock, and 25 percent Turface.

Getting Started Nursery stock, air layers, or cuttings are all excellent choices. It may also be fun and relatively easy to collect an already woody vine from a garden and start training it into a bonsai.

Styling

Pruning To keep it well shaped, prune the vine back to two sets of leaves—English ivy can take a hard pruning to encourage an abundance of branches. Use wire to position the new growth. Stake and wire a young plant to develop an upright form. Focus primarily on developing a strong trunk and keeping the plant's sprawling tendencies in check.

Wiring This vine is pliable and can be wired at any time, making it a great choice for neophyte bonsai artists.

Recommended Styles English ivy is a natural for a cascade. It can also be trained in the informal upright style, but it's not suited for formal upright. *—R.M.*

Myrtus communis | Myrtle

The small dark and glossy evergreen leaves and the rough bark the tree develops with age make myrtle an ideal candidate for bonsai all year long, but during summer it also explodes with exquisite white flowers that resemble fireworks bursting in the night sky. A profusion of long stamens protruding from the flowers is responsible for the grand show. An evergreen shrub that grows to about ten feet tall and seven to eight feet wide, myrtle can be found growing from southern Europe to northern Africa, where it prefers coastal areas.

Growing

Light From late spring through summer, grow myrtle outdoors since it needs plenty of light to flower abundantly. But place it in semi-shade during the hot midday sun in summer.

Temperature Range Myrtles grow happily at 70°F to 85°F and should be placed on a humidity tray or misted occasionally to emulate their Mediterranean coastal environment. In fall move the tree inside when the weather drops to 55°F. Though the species can withstand lower temperatures, it will acclimate better to the indoors if it is moved in at 55°F or warmer.

Watering In spring and summer when growth is strongest, myrtles may use a lot of water, so monitor your tree's require-ments carefully and increase watering as needed. Do not overwater; the roots will rot if the soil is constantly wet. To keep them from fading and dropping, never wet the flowers. Fertilize myrtle with a well-balanced fertilizer at half strength once a week in spring and summer. In fall and winter, fertilize every two to three weeks as long as temperatures are kept above 55°F. Stop fertilizing just before and during flowering (otherwise you'll encourage vegetative growth). After flowering, resume fertilizing as in spring and summer.

Repotting Repot in spring every two to three years.

Recommended Soil Blend Use fast-draining bonsai soil.

Getting Started Propagate from seeds or cuttings.

Specimen above: informal upright, 8 inches tall

Styling

Pruning In spring and summer, pruning is necessary to keep this species' growth in check, which is especially strong from the bottom. Cut suckers emerging at the base of the trunk to keep the bonsai's strength equally distributed. In the early stages of training, let branches grow to six inches, then cut back to two or three leaves. After basic branch shaping is achieved, clip new growth back to two leaves once four sets of leaves have emerged. Stop pruning during flowering or if growth stops during winter rest. When flowers are spent, resume pruning. With mature bonsai this is a good time to open up the foliage to allow in more light.

Wiring Use aluminum wire to avoid damaging the thin bark. You can wire branches that are up to three years old, but the older the branch, the less movement it will allow. Cut older branches back and shape with wire the pliable new growth that emerges.

Recommended Styles Myrtles can be groomed into most bonsai styles. —*J.V.*

Olea europaea | European Olive

Olives are extremely popular bonsai in Europe and elsewhere, with many ancient masterpieces developed from wild-collected specimens. With rough gray bark and small narrow oval leaves, olives are suited to all sizes and styles of bonsai, and people who enjoy the sculptured look of weathered wood among the foliage will be well satisfied with this species. Native to the coastal areas of the eastern Mediterranean region, olives have been cultivated for millennia, primarily for oil. Evergreens reaching 30 to 40 feet tall, they can easily live hundreds of years, and some specimens are reputedly more than a thousand years old. The leaves have adapted to prevent transpiration during periods of drought, which may account in part for the tree's longevity.

Specimen above: clump style, 20 inches tall and 24 inches wide, about 150 years old and in training as a bonsai for 30 years

Growing

Light Full sun is best for the olive. Keep it outside during spring and summer if possible. Indoors, good southern or western exposure is essential for vigorous growth.

Temperature Range The olive can handle cool temperatures, but as a bonsai, keep it above 45°F; 70°F to 85°F is optimal in spring and summer.

Watering Adapted to living with drought, olives prefer it if the soil dries out somewhat between watering. This helps keep their root system healthy. In spring and summer, fertilize every week with a balanced fertilizer at half strength. In fall and winter, reduce it to every two to three weeks if temperatures are kept above 55°F.

Repotting Repot every two to three years. Olives handle root work with no problem, tolerating the removal of 30 percent of hair roots easily.

Recommended Soil Blend Fast-draining bonsai soil is good for olives.

Getting Started The species propagates from seeds and cuttings.

Styling

Pruning During active growth, prune starting in spring. When working with branches on a young tree, let the shoots grow, then cut them back to two or three leaves to force buds that sit farther back on the branches to grow, thus promoting good branching. Once the tree has developed its basic branch structure, pinch back new growth: As soon as new shoots have grown seven to eight leaves, cut them back to two or three leaves to create a dense, full look. Continue this regimen during the growing season, but stop during the winter rest period.

Wiring Branches should be wired when they are still young and flexible. By the time they are two or three years old, they become brittle and tend to snap when wiring is attempted. Wire and position a young branch, let it grow, and then cut it back part of the way. Repeat this procedure until you have achieved the desired branch movement.

Recommended Styles Olives can be designed in most major styles, perhaps with the exception of exposed root style, although nature has a way of surprising us. —*J.V.*

Osmanthus fragrans | Tea Olive

As its botanical name suggests, tea olive has extremely fragrant clusters of small flowers. Forming from fall to spring, the flowers range in color from white to shades of yellow and stand against a backdrop of shiny dark green oval leaves and attractive gray bark. Tea olive is a slow-growing evergreen shrub native to China and Japan that grows to around 30 feet but adapts well to container cultivation. It prefers full to partial sun.

Growing

Light Tea olive likes a sunny or well-lit spot. Summer the tree outdoors.

Temperature Range For optimal growth, keep this plant at 70°F to 85°F in spring through summer, dropping to 60°F to 65°F in winter.

Watering Keep the soil slightly moist to dry—but not too dry. Fertilize weekly with a well-balanced fertilizer at half strength during active growth, and in fall and winter every two to three weeks if temperatures are kept above 55°F. Tea olive likes a slightly acidic soil, so applying an acidic fertilizer formulated for azaleas or camellias at half strength once a month during active growth only will help keep the tree happy.

Repotting Repot every three to four years.

Recommended Soil Blend Pot in normal fast-draining bonsai soil. Add a small amount of chopped New Zealand sphagnum peat moss to the soil to increase soil acidity.

Getting Started Propagate this plant through cuttings.

Styling

Pruning While developing the shape of the tree, prune new growth back to two sets of leaves. Note that in so doing you will remove the buds for the fragrant flowers along the way. Prune mature tea olive in early summer, since it flowers from fall to spring on the tips of hardened growth. Prune fresh growth back to two leaves in strong areas and to four

Specimen above: informal upright, 18 inches tall

leaves on slightly weaker growth. Always prune back to healthy leaves that have visibly healthy dormant buds at the base of the leaf. After this pruning, let the branches grow freely in order to flower. During flowering, plant growth is minimal, and no pruning will be necessary. After flowering, a very light pruning can be done, then do not prune again until the following summer.

Wiring The branches of this plant remain flexible, so wiring can be done at any time.

Recommended Styles Tea olive is most suited for multitrunk and informal upright styles. —*J.V.*

Podocarpus macrophyllus
Chinese Podocarpus

Also known as Buddhist pine, this conifer is a great bonsai for lovers of classical forms. Its thin upward-pointing leaves are whorled around the branches, giving it a look that's very similar to yew foliage. With the right care, the enthusiast can design all the great conifer shapes, such as formal and informal upright. Native to southern China, this is a slow-growing evergreen shrub that usually grows about 15 to 20 feet tall. It prefers somewhat mild to warm environments with good yearly rainfall.

Specimen above: semi-cascade, 16 1/2 inches tall, about 50 years old and in training for 25 years

Growing

Light Outdoors, Chinese podocarpus does just fine in light shade; indoors, it prefers bright light.

Temperature Range This bonsai can handle fairly cool weather, and fall and winter temperatures can drop without any harm to about 45°F. It prefers highs of 70°F to 85°F in spring and summer.

Watering Keep the soil slightly moist at all times. Be careful not to overwater to avoid weakening the roots and causing discoloration of the foliage. Fertilize weekly with a balanced fertilizer at half strength. In fall and winter, fertilize once every two to three weeks as long as temperatures are kept above 55°F. Podocarpus likes slightly acidic soil, which you can simulate by fertilizing at half strength with a fertilizer for azaleas or camellias. Use the acidic fertilizer once per month during active growth, then stop during winter.

Repotting Every three to five years, repot, taking extra care when working with the roots. This species is sensitive and does not like aggressive root pruning. Remove only 10 to 15 percent.

Recommended Soil Blend Fast-draining bonsai soil works well, with a very small amount of chopped sphagnum peat moss added to the soil to increase acidity.

Getting Started It is best to propagate this tree from a cutting.

Styling

Pruning During active growth, prune anytime. In the early design stages, letting branches grow for some time, then cutting back to new buds that are relatively close to the trunk will help develop nice branch taper and quicken branch development. After the basic structure is set, prune buds as they elongate in spring, leaving four or five new leaves. This will promote plenty of bud development farther back on the branches and create a nice full look. Even though this tree is a relatively slow grower, it's good to keep up with this regimen to encourage dense foliage rather than long leggy growth.

Wiring Wire branches when they are still young and flexible. Once they harden, they become brittle and may snap. Once branches harden, use clip-and-grow directional pruning.

Recommended Styles Podocarpus can be styled in all classical forms. For a natural feel, try one popular for conifers, such as informal upright. —*J.V.*

Psidium littorale | Cattley Guava

This tropical plant has small, delicate white flowers with multiple stamens that lead to beautiful and edible red fruit. The tree has smooth, flaky light brown bark, somewhat large dark green alternate oval leaves, and new spring growth in a nice shade of red. Its large leaves make it a great species for midsize to large bonsai. Cattley guava is a shrub or small tree native to Brazil and grows about 10 to 18 feet tall. It can grow in a wide range of semi-moist soil conditions.

Growing

Light Place guava in a well-lit area for healthy growth. If grown inside all year, place it near a western-facing window with good sunlight. Use grow-lights if good light exposure is not available.

Temperature Range In spring through summer, grow the tree at 80°F to 90°F. For prolific flowering in late spring to early summer, this guava needs the shorter days of fall and winter with temperatures around 65°F to 70°F. It is best to grow this tree outside during late spring through summer. Move it back indoors when nighttime temps fall to 68°F to 70°F. It can tolerate cooler temperatures but will acclimate to the indoors better if it is brought in before it gets too cool.

Watering Water as needed to keep the soil slightly moist. Fertilize once a week with a well-balanced fertilizer in spring. Stop just before flowering starts, and don't fertilize again until the fruit has matured. When growth slows in winter, fertilize once a month at half strength until spring.

Repotting Repot every two to three years. The best time to do it is after fruiting, but you can also repot in spring before flowering. Cattley guava can handle root pruning well, tolerating the removal of 30 percent of the hair root mass easily.

Recommended Soil Blend Pot in normal fast-draining bonsai soil.

Getting Started It is best to propagate by seed or cuttings.

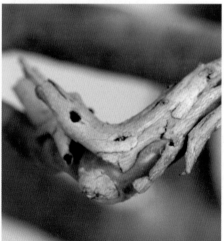

Specimen above: twin trunk style, 24 inches tall

Styling

Pruning Because of its substantial leaf and fruit size, Cattley guava looks best and stays healthiest if styled in an open shape. To create compact but open growth that keeps the leaves from shading each other, prune the tree back to healthy shoots after fruiting in summer. New buds will develop farther back on the branches. The following spring, use these new shoots to create compact growth.

Wiring Anytime of the year is suitable for wiring the tree.

Recommended Styles This tree works best for informal upright and windswept styles. *—J.V.*

Rosmarinus officinalis
Common Rosemary

Rosemary is a great bonsai for all kinds of enthusiasts: people who appreciate interesting bark textures, because it quickly grows a rough-fissured, ancient-looking trunk; flower lovers, who can enjoy its profuse small blue flowers from spring through summer; and people who value the well-known wonderful aroma the narrow leaves give off. For stylists, the small-size leaves and tight growth as well as its vigor make rosemary suitable for all sizes and styles of bonsai. In its native habitat in the Mediterranean region, the perennial shrub grows about three to five feet high and wide.

Specimen above: informal upright, 15 inches tall and 13 1/2 inches wide, about 30 years old and in training as a bonsai for 3 years

Growing

Light Rosemary likes sunny growing conditions with low humidity. It's ideal for a bright sunlit window and the low humidity levels commonly found indoors.

Temperature Range Keep rosemary at 70°F to 80°F in spring and summer and around 60°F to 65°F during winter.

Watering Rosemary does not like its roots constantly moist. Water only as needed, letting the soil dry out somewhat in between. During peak growth in the summer's heat, water more, but make sure the plant really needs it before pulling out the watering can. Fertilize weekly with a balanced fertilizer at half strength during spring and summer. In fall and winter, once every two to three weeks will do. Even though growth does slow, it will continue to grow in winter, and a little fertilizer will keep it healthy.

Repotting Every two years in mid- to late spring, it's time to repot. Rosemary's roots grow very fast and can handle root pruning with no problems. In the year that you repot, prune some branches to balance top growth with root growth.

Recommended Soil Blend Pot using a fast-draining bonsai medium to keep the soil from staying wet for too long.

Getting Started Propagate rosemary through cuttings.

Styling

Pruning Common rosemary is a vigorous grower that slows down considerably in winter but doesn't stop. For bonsai in development, let branches grow long, then prune them back. On mature trees, pruning should be done to maintain the profile of the shaped bonsai and to create denser branching. Rosemary develops new growth easily and abundantly from buds that sit farther back on the branches. Use this characteristic to develop branches with good movement and taper with the clip-and-grow method.

Wiring Wire branches while they are still flexible, up to two years old. Once branches harden, they tend to be brittle. Use wire to set basic branch positions and curvature, then use clip-and-grow directional pruning to further shape branches. This bonsai develops nice dense branches surprisingly quickly.

Recommended Styles Rosemary can be styled in most bonsai styles. —J.V.

Serissa japonica | Serissa

This serissa is a flower lover's delight. Few other bonsai can offer a profusion of small perfect flowers that please almost all year; and if flowers are not enough, it has very rough tan bark that quickly gives the impression of age. Because of its small leaf and flower size, this species can be designed and grown in all sizes, including *mame* (extra-small trees). Serissa can be a bit finicky. It does not like to be moved from one environment to another; it prefers instead to stay in one spot and adapt to it. Once comfortable, serissa will grow well and strong. A change of light source or temperature may cause flower drop and yellowing, dropping leaves. Native to China, Japan, and India, *Serissa japonica*, formerly known as *S. foetida*, is a small evergreen shrub that grows in moist wooded areas, where it reaches about three to four feet tall and wide. It thrives in mild to warm, humid environments.

Growing

Light Give serissa bright light and keep it in the same place all year long.

Temperature Range During the growing season, spring and summer, 70°F to 85°F is ideal. Serissa can take low temperatures of about 60°F to 65°F during fall and winter.

Watering Keep the soil slightly moist. Don't wet the flowers because they will discolor, then rot. Keep humidity levels high by placing the tree on a tray filled with gravel and water, or mist the bonsai a few times a day, keeping the flowers as dry as possible. Don't panic if your tree drops some leaves occasionally. Just be aware that it may need less water when this happens. Fertilize once a week with a balanced fertilizer at half strength in spring and summer. In fall and winter, fertilize every two to three weeks.

Repotting To help keep the roots healthy without forcing you to cut too much of the root ball at one time, repot every year or two. Root prune lightly, about ten percent—the species is prone to dropping leaves if you remove more.

Specimen above: informal upright, 3 inches tall

Recommended Soil Blend Fast-draining bonsai soil is best for serissa.

Getting Started Propagating from cuttings works well.

Styling

Pruning Serissa is an extremely fast grower that takes well to hard pruning, sending out an abundance of new growth. Constant tip pruning as branches extend and flowers start to wither will keep the in shape and also promote denser growth close to the bases of branches and good flower development. Despite vigilant pruning, branches can become so dense that they impede sunlight from reaching interior ones. When this occurs, prune hard to open up the canopy and invigorate lower branches.

Wiring Before branches harden during active growth, wiring should be done on new soft growth. Clip and grow after the basic branch structure is achieved.

Recommended Styles Suitable for most classical forms, serissa lends itself to root over rock or exposed root styles because it easily develops low aerial roots. *—J. V.*

Syzygium paniculatum | Brush Cherry

This shrub produces abundant small dark shiny green leaves that work well with small to medium bonsai. It has small white powder-puff flowers that are occasionally followed by red fruit resembling cherries. Small-leafed cultivars are especially popular for bonsai. The tree, formerly known as *Eugenia paniculata*, is native to Australia and generally grows to about 12 to 18 feet.

Specimen above: informal upright, 26 inches tall

Growing

Light Brush cherry needs bright light: Keep it in a window with southern or western exposure or supplement with grow-lights.

Temperature Range Cool winters (inside) are preferred, approximately 55°F to 65°F. An average of about 70°F to 85°F is good for the rest of the year. Summer it outdoors and move back inside when nighttime temperatures drop to the mid-50s.

Watering Keep the soil evenly moist and fertilize weekly with a balanced fertilizer at half strength; reduce fertilizing to once every two to three weeks in winter.

Repotting Repot annually during the active growing season. This tree produces a lot of fibrous roots, so be sure to take off a third of the root ball.

Recommended Soil Blend A good combination is 60 percent Metro mix 510, 15 percent lava rock, 25 percent Turface.

Getting Started For beginners it's recommended to start with nursery stock, soft wood cuttings collected during active growth, or air layers. Look for a specimen with small leaves about an inch long. The cultivar 'Teenie Genie' is popular with bonsai artists because of its compact growth and much smaller leaves, only about a quarter-inch long.

Styling

Pruning To develop the shape of this tree, cut it back hard and remove all or most of the foliage. Pruning hard generates good growth from lots of buds. Removing the foliage allows light into the interior, promoting bud development close to the core of the tree, which is very helpful to encourage dense branching and a sturdy trunk. Do major pruning in the early summer months when the tree grows most vigorously. To maintain the shape of the tree, prune back new growth regularly.

Wiring This species can be wired anytime during the year. Its branches are fairly flexible, and the tree is easy to work with. Just be mindful of its thorns.

Recommended Styles Informal upright and forest styles are both good for brush cherry. —*R.M.*

Trachelospermum asiaticum
Asian Jasmine

This evergreen vine is easy to work with, making it a nice small bonsai for beginners. Its leaves are oval, approximately one to two inches long, and a glossy dark green. The pale yellow blooms are small but highly fragrant and only appear on mature specimens. As its name implies, it is native to Southeast Asia.

Growing

Light Bright light is preferred, with a southern or western window exposure or grow-lights.

Temperature Range Asian jasmine prefers cool winters (inside), approximately 55°F to 65°F; the rest of the time, a good average is 70°F to 85°F. It also does well outside during the growing season.

Watering Keep the soil evenly moist. Fertilize weekly with a balanced fertilizer at half strength; reduce to once every two to three weeks in winter. Supplement once a month with an acidic fertilizer at half strength.

Repotting Every two years the plant can be repotted, but be careful of cutting the roots back too harshly—trim them about half an inch all around.

Recommended Soil Blend It likes slightly acidic soil. A good combination is 50 percent Metro mix 510, 25 percent lava rock, and 25 percent Turface.

Getting Started Cuttings and air layers are best for beginners.

Styling

Pruning When you train the bonsai into a cascade style, prune this vine hard to encourage plentiful branching. Cut back new growth to two sets of leaves to keep the mature bonsai in shape. Prune

Specimen above: cascade, 32 inches from highest to lowest point

back hard to develop a strong trunk for an upright style. Sacrifice the flowers while the plant is young and in development. Prune mature specimens after flowering in spring to early summer.

Wiring As a vine, Asian jasmine makes a nice cascade-style bonsai. It needs to be staked as well as wired to develop a woody trunk strong enough to support an upright style. The plant's growth pattern is erratic and it doesn't hold its shape easily, but it is rather pliable. Set the initial shape with wires, and remove them after one year. Let the bonsai rest for six months, then rewire it.

Recommended Styles Cascade works very well with the plant's natural habit, but the informal upright style can also be achieved. *—R.M.*

Ulmus parvifolia | Chinese Elm

Chinese elm is a classic example of a deciduous bonsai and one of the few trees in that category adaptable for indoor growing. The many cultivars generally belong in one of two groups. Cultivars with rough bark tend to be hardier and should be grown outdoors. Cultivars with smooth bark can be grown outdoors year-round but can also handle growing indoors year-round. Chinese elm can be an evergreen if kept indoors with warm temperatures, but it is best for the longevity of the tree to give it some sort of rest period with lower temperatures during winter indoors. The cooler its winter area, the more leaves drop. This is normal and will keep the bonsai vigorous. A fast grower with small oval leaves, this tree is suitable for all bonsai sizes. It is native in northern China, Japan, Korea, and northern Vietnam and grows to a height of about 50 feet. Many cultivars used for bonsai grow shorter.

Specimen above: broom style, 22 inches tall

Growing

Light When grown indoors, place Chinese elm in a well-lit or sunny area. The tree benefits from a summer spent outdoors.

Temperature Range In spring through summer, growing temperatures of 70°F to 85°F are ideal. If possible, lower temperature to 60°F to 65°F during winter.

Watering Chinese elm likes the soil kept slightly moist, but overwatering can cause root problems, so be vigilant. Add a balanced fertilizer at half strength every week in spring and summer and every two to three weeks in fall and winter if temperatures are kept above 60°F.

Repotting Repot in early spring every other year. Roots grow quickly and strongly, so aggressive root pruning is a good idea. Take off a good third of the hair roots.

Recommended Soil Blend Planting in normal fast-draining bonsai soil will help control overwatering. Prune branches after the tree has recovered from repotting to balance foliage and root mass.

Getting Started Dwarf cultivars best suited for bonsai are grown from cuttings.

Styling

Pruning During winter, growth will slow down or stop, depending on indoor temperatures, but the strong growth habit and alternating leaf pattern of Chinese elm makes well-shaped branching easy to achieve, and pruning may be done most of the year. In early stages of development, let branches grow freely to thicken and gain strength, and then cut back hard to two or three leaves. Continue this process to develop tapered branches. The clip-and-grow method works particularly well because the tree grows alternating leaves, simplifying the process. Simply pick a leaf pointing in the direction you want the branch to grow and prune right above that leaf. When three or four leaves have developed, pinching back new tender growth to one or two leaves will cause the buds farther back to develop, making for dense, full branches.

Wiring Though it can be done at any time, wiring is best done when branches are under one year old and flexible during active growth in spring and summer. Branches quickly grow and harden into shape.

Recommended Styles Chinese elm can be designed in most major styles. —J.V.

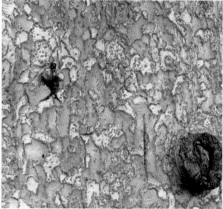

Bonsai require diligent care. Monitor the trees closely and check their needs on a daily basis to provide proper ventilation, humidity, and water.

Indoor Bonsai Care

Jerry Meislik

Growing bonsai indoors requires some basic horticultural knowledge and a good dose of diligence to provide the trees with an environment in which they can thrive. For starters, selecting species suitable for indoor growing is of paramount importance. Like many other plants, bonsai do best when cultivated in conditions that are similar to those found in the native habitats of the individual tree species. That's why pines and junipers as well as other trees native to cold-temperate climates do not usually survive for long in the average centrally heated home. They require a cool resting period each year—exactly at the time when people living in cold climates crank up their thermostats and heat their homes to a balmy 70 degrees Fahrenheit or more. However, the bonsai enthusiast who doesn't command a cool greenhouse can choose from a number of mostly tropical and subtropical trees, such as those featured in the encyclopedia, which are all suited to cultivation in centrally heated quarters. And provided the trees receive the right amount of water, enough light, and good all-around care, they should do well in the somewhat plant-hostile indoor environment.

Ventilation and Humidity

Green plants require carbon dioxide for photosynthesis and oxygen for their other chemical processes. When light is available, plants produce more oxygen than they use. The excess oxygen that they release is used by nearly all living things on earth. Plants also produce carbon dioxide throughout the day and night.

Since both carbon dioxide and oxygen are critical to good plant growth, it is important to circulate the air so that its component gases are freely available to bonsai. A small electric fan set nearby—but not directly at—the trees is very helpful in maintaining good air flow. It is also an effective way to keep insect pests and fungal diseases in check. (For more tips on disease and pest prevention, see page 108.)

Humidity in many modern homes can drop to seriously low levels when the heat is on in winter or the air conditioner is running full blast in summer. Cacti and succulents can grow and flourish in low-humidity environments, but most other plants are healthier and grow more vigorously if the humidity is higher; for example, a growing area that has a humidity level averaging 30 percent or above should be acceptable for most tropical and subtropical bonsai. In general, plants with thick, waxy leaves like a rubbery-leafed fig (*Ficus* species) or Natal plum (*Carissa macrocarpa*) tolerate dry air the best, and plants with thin leaves like a serissa easily dry out in low humidity.

Healthy Humidity Levels

Cool Surroundings One approach to increasing relative humidity during the heating period is to keep the room where your plants live cooler than the rest of your home. During the warmer months, keep the air conditioning, which removes moisture from the air, off or at a low level.

Misting Frequent misting helps to temporarily raise the humidity level in the growing area, but it is often impractical and may increase the chances of a disease outbreak. Most of these diseases are fungal and can be seen as brown or black spots on the central area of the leaves, withering branches, or wet, oozing areas on the bark.

Gravel-Filled Water Trays Add water almost to the surface of the gravel in the tray and set the tray near or under the plants to slightly increase humidity levels around the plants. Never place plant pots directly in water, but rather keep them elevated above the water line.

Humidifiers Cool and warm air humidifiers work equally well when placed close to the plants.

Grow Tent A simple frame covered by clear plastic and surrounding the growing area is used by many successful indoor gardeners to increase the humidity around plants. Never seal the plants completely in plastic, as fungi can then become a problem.

Watering Bonsai

Improper watering is probably to blame for the demise of more bonsai than any other problem. Trees in very small containers (less than four inches long), for example, are easily overlooked and may miss out on watering, which can easily lead to their death. Water is critical for the survival of all living things, and bonsai are no exception. The fine hair, or fibrous, roots responsible for every bonsai's water uptake must never be allowed to completely dry out, nor can they be kept continually wet. Hair roots kept immersed in water will rot since they need oxygen to survive. (Gases, including oxygen, diffuse through water 10,000 times less easily than through air.) Water-saturated soil deprives hair roots of the oxygen vital to their metabolic processes. Either too dry or too wet a situation will result in the death of the hair roots and, quickly thereafter, the rest of the plant.

Water Quality

Water quality is an important factor in keeping bonsai thriving. In most municipalities tap water is fine for bonsai culture, but if you notice salt and mineral crusts building up on the soil surface and around the rims of your pots, the mineral content of the water is quite possibly too high for your bonsai. If your plants show yellow leaves, darker green veins, and generally poor leaf color, the water may be too hard, or mineral-laden. Check with the water board of your municipality, or send a water sample off for testing to your local county agricultural extension service.

Tap Water and Rainwater If your tap water is too hard, this may be signaled by off-color leaves (chlorosis), browning edges on leaves, or misshapen leaves. Instead, you can use rainwater, water collected by a dehumidifier, air conditioner, or furnace, or water from a reverse-osmosis filtration system. Water from these sources is low in salt and ideal for growing most plants. This type of water is not suitable for trees that are "lime loving." If you only use water from these sources you must use a complete fertilizer, one that contains all major, minor, and trace elements. (For more on fertilizers, see page 84.)

Frequency of Watering

				WATER MORE			
Coarse soil	Small pot	Sunny	Warm	Windy	Young tree	Actively growing	Not repotted
				WATER LESS			
Fine soil	Large pot	Shade	Cool	Calm	Older tree	Dormant	Newly repotted

Adjust the soil mix and watering schedule to compensate for these variables.

Check every bonsai at least once a day to determine if it needs water. When watering, allow moisture to thoroughly soak the soil and then run out of the pot's drain holes.

Watering Technique and Timing

To determine whether it's time to water your bonsai, gently probe the soil about one inch below the soil surface with a finger. If the soil feels almost dry, the bonsai needs to be watered. Allow water to penetrate the soil until it is completely wet and excess water runs out of the drain holes of the pot. Allow the soil to become nearly dry before watering again.

Proper Timing For most trees, soil and growing conditions are correct if the tree needs water every 24 to 36 hours. If the soil is staying wet longer than 36 to 48 hours, the potting soil may be too fine for your growing conditions. Or it may be old and broken down to very fine, water-retentive particles. Either way, the tree should be repotted right away or only lightly watered (in such a way that it dries in 36 hours or less) until the soil can be changed. (See "Repotting," page 92, for details.)

Proper Watering Technique Allow moisture to thoroughly soak the soil, and then allow it to drain out of the hole in the bottom of the pot. Many growers put their bonsai temporarily into a sink or basin to catch the excess water.

If this sounds like a lot of watering, consider the alternatives. In order to be watered less frequently, your tree would have to grow in a more water-retentive soil mix, achievable with finer soil particles and a higher proportion of organic matter. But the longer the soil stays wet the slimmer the chances that your tree will thrive. Conversely, by decreasing the percentage of organic materials and/or increasing the soil particle size, you have to water more frequently, but your tree stands a much better chance of having a long and healthy life.

Fertilizing Bonsai

Given adequate amounts of light, plants synthesize all that they need from water, carbon dioxide, oxygen, and minerals, which are either found in the soil or added to it in the form of fertilizer. Fertilizers contain the major and minor minerals that plants require. Prominently displayed on fertilizer bottles and packages are the three letters NPK, followed by three numbers. These indicate how much of the major minerals, or macronutrients—nitrogen, phosphorus, and potassium—the product contains. For example, a ten-pound bag with the listing 20-20-20 contains two pounds each of nitrogen, phosphorus, and potassium and four pounds of inert filler. Many fertilizers also contain minor minerals, or micronutrients, such as sulfur, calcium, and magnesium. Some also contain trace elements like boron, chloride, cobalt, copper, iron manganese, molybdenum, and zinc. Package inserts supplied with all fertilizers describe exactly what components are contained in a fertilizer.

Fertilizer Components

COMPONENTS	MINERALS
Macro (major)	nitrogen, phosphorus, potassium
Micro (minor)	calcium, magnesium, sulfur
Trace	boron, chloride, cobalt, copper, iron, manganese, molybdenum, zinc

Types of Fertilizers

Organic Fertilizers Derived from plant or animal sources, they are generally considered safer to use than inorganic fertilizers since they must be broken down to simple chemicals by heat, moisture, bacteria, and fungi in the soil before they slowly begin to release nutrients. It is thus more difficult to "overdose" or "burn" roots with organic fertilizers. On the downside, organic fertilizers decompose and may attract insects, molds, and bacteria, and give off unpleasant odors in the process. These attributes make organic fertilizers much less suitable for indoor use than for outdoor use. However, if you summer your trees outside, a mixture of organic fertilizer components formed into a small cake ($1^{1}/_{2}$ to 2 inches in diameter) and placed on top of the soil may be a useful option. Try a blend of bone, blood, fish, and kelp meal, bonded with fish emulsion. By varying the ingredients and proportions you can adjust the homemade fertilizer blend to the needs of individual trees.

Inorganic Fertilizers Salts that when diluted in water are immediately available to plants, they must be applied with care because it's easy to use too much of them. However, they are relatively odorless and don't attract insects and so are the mainstay for fertilizing indoor bonsai collections.

Long-Acting Inorganic Fertilizers Also known as slow-acting or timed-release fertilizers, these are pellets of inorganic chemicals coated in resin. The resin allows the fertilizer to be gradually released to the plant depending on moisture and/or temperature. Long-acting fertilizers are formulated to be effective for weeks or months. They may degrade as they age and cause a spurt of chemical to be released to the plant all at once, causing root burn that could harm or even kill a tree. If you notice dust while handling a long-acting fertilizer, it may indicate damaged resin coating. In this state, the fertilizer is not safe for bonsai. (You can still use it in the garden, though you may want to avoid applying inorganic fertilizers near vegetables and herbs.) As with any chemical, avoid breathing in dust and avoid skin exposure.

Applying Fertilizer

How often you need to fertilize depends largely on the composition of the soil blend and the growth phase of your tree. Inorganic growing media require fertilizer more often than organic soils since the organic materials in soil hold onto nutrients much better than inorganic media do. Organic soil components have a high cation-exchange capacity, or CEC, which allows nutrients to remain in the soil for some time. They also contain humic acid and beneficial bacteria and fungi. Inorganic soil components have a low CEC and relatively poor ability to hold fertilizer constituents in the soil. When you use largely or completely inorganic soil mixes, fertilize more frequently. Be sure to thoroughly drench the soil with water before fertilizing your trees to avoid harming the roots.

Dosing If you choose a commercial inorganic fertilizer like Miracle-Gro, Miracid, Peters, or Schultz's, apply it at half the recommended strength. Inorganic fertilizers are very potent, and if overused, will force the plant to grow more than is beneficial for its long-term health or beauty. Frequently alternate between products to vary the minor and trace minerals offered to your bonsai. Use the much less potent and much slower acting organic fertilizers at full strength. Amazingly, bonsai will do well if not fertilized for months. They can survive for a year or more without fertilizer, so err on the side of caution. A conservative fertilizing schedule will result in healthier and more vigorous bonsai.

During the Growing Season Fertilize actively growing trees potted in largely inorganic soil mixes (made up of lava rock, chicken grit, Turface, and the like) once to twice a week. Fertilize trees in soil mixes containing 50 percent or more organic components (such as peat moss or bark chips) once every week or two.

During the Resting Period Reduce fertilization to once per month when the bonsai is not in active growth. Never fertilize a sick tree—fertilizer may kill it. It is also best to wait two to three weeks after repotting a tree to fertilize it.

No matter what blend you use, sift all growing media to remove small particles that would make the soil too water retentive.

Growing Media

A properly composed growing medium containing organic and inorganic ingredients keeps your plants healthy and maintenance to a minimum. Soil provides moisture, gases, and minerals as well as physical support for your plants. Over time a soil's characteristics change: The organic components break down to smaller-sized particles; the inorganic components remain more stable. The finer particles compromise adequate gaseous exchange and drainage. Gradually the soil becomes less porous and more water retentive. The composition of your soil mix determines how long it stays viable. Soil that contains organic materials needs to be replaced more frequently than soil composed exclusively of inorganic components. If you notice that the soil in a bonsai pot starts staying wet longer after a thorough watering, it's time to replace it.

The Right Blend

Depending on their components, soil blends vary in pH, CEC (cation-exchange capacity), bacterial and fungal composition, fertility, and many other factors too numerous to list. Most growers use a mix of organic and inorganic ingredients. There is no one ideal soil mix, and even experienced growers are continually tinkering with their mixes to adjust for varying factors specific to their trees and growing conditions.

Some add fungal spores (mycorrhizae), trace elements, long-acting fertilizers, vitamin B12, hormones, and other agents. Other growers may prefer a growing medium that contains just one soil component, such as red-lava particles.

Soil pH The acidity or alkalinity of the soil is difficult to measure and to control accurately over time. Luckily, most plant species tolerate a fairly wide pH range, from about 6 to 8, without showing any evidence of growth problems. Acid-loving plants such as azaleas and other ericaceous plants like a low pH, or acidic soil, which can be achieved with the addition of sphagnum peat moss or sulfur. Alkaline- or lime-loving trees do well when watered from most municipal water systems and wells because these tend to provide water that's somewhat alkaline.

Chlorosis This condition, revealed by yellowing leaves and darker veins, indicates an imbalance in the pH or mineral content in the soil mix. Checking pH can be done most easily with pH indicator (litmus) paper, available at most nurseries. A portion of the soil mix is moistened with pH-neutral water (roughly pH 7), and then measured with a test strip that turns various colors that indicate the pH of the soil. Another tool, the pH meter, does not work well for most bonsai soils since the soils' particular granular quality makes testing nearly impossible. Other mineral imbalances are difficult to detect without submitting your soil to a sophisticated chemical analysis.

Commercial and Homemade Soil Blends

Sift Before You Pot No matter what soil materials you choose, sift each ingredient over a window screen or fine sieve and use only the material that stays on top. This single step can help you grow bonsai more successfully. The fine material that falls through the screen may be used in your garden but never in bonsai soil.

Commercial Soil Blends for Bonsai The simplest option for obtaining the proper soil, a commercial bonsai potting mix should not be used straight out of the bag; sift it first, as instructed above. The bags often contain particles that are very fine, and these small-sized particles will hold moisture far too long. Never use regular potting soil.

Homemade Soil Blends If you want to make your own blend, a mixture of one half sifted bonsai potting soil and one half chicken grit ($1/16$-inch to $3/8$-inch particles), red lava, or even aquarium or other gravel is a good start. This simple blend holds moisture quite well and creates pore spaces that allow air to get to the roots. Small bark chips (sold as orchid seedling bark, $1/8$-inch to $3/8$-inch size) can be substituted for the bonsai potting soil to make an even more airy mix. If you are ready for more tinkering, take a look at the list of organic and inorganic soil components that follows. It is easy to mix your own bonsai blend to your requirements. The properties of your growing medium depend in large part on the size and nature of the particles you mix and can be adjusted to best serve the needs of the plant that you are growing in it.

Common Organic Soil Components
(all contain some nutrients)

Bark Chips Hold moisture and minerals. They break down gradually over time. Chips should be small, about $1/8$- to $3/8$-inch square.

Cocoa Hulls Not suited for bonsai. Cocoa hulls are too moisture retentive and break down very easily. (They are also toxic to dogs, who are attracted by their chocolate aroma.)

Decomposed Leaves Contain minerals and microorganisms. Break down easily and may harbor diseases.

Peat Moss Holds moisture; is acidic, antifungal, and antibacterial. It may become water repellent with age. Canadian sphagnum peat moss can be used as a soil component. New Zealand sphagnum peat moss is suitable for air layering (page 107). Or use it on the soil surface after repotting to retain moisture and provide antiseptic properties.

Pine Needles Hold moisture and minerals and are acidic. They break down gradually; may harbor diseases.

Inorganic Soil Components
(contain no nutrients)

Akadama A reddish granular mineral mined in Japan, akadama is available in different grades and sizes. It is a common bonsai-growing medium in Japan; expensive in North America. It provides excellent moisture-air balance. Can stay too wet if used alone.

Chicken or Turkey Grit Promotes good drainage. Heavy in weight. Colors vary widely.

Crushed Lava Rock (often red) Promotes good drainage. Lighter in weight than other stone.

Decomposed Granite Promotes good drainage. Heavy in weight. Colors vary.

Components of bonsai soil, from top to bottom: bark chips, Canadian sphagnum peat moss, New Zealand sphagnum peat moss, akadama, lava rock, and Turface.

Gravel Promotes good drainage.

Kanuma Of mineral origin and, like akadama, a popular medium in Japan, where it is mined. Particularly useful for acid-loving plants like azaleas and camellias.

Sand Coarse construction sand is best; beach sand is too fine and salty.

Turface The trade name of a high-grade calcined clay product commonly used by the horticulture industry. Provides good drainage and allows for fine root growth without adding a lot of weight.

Other Inorganic Materials River stone, decomposed granite, and haydite (expanded shale aggregate) are examples of materials available in some areas of the country that can be successfully used in bonsai soil mix. May be readily available in your local area and can be used instead of costly materials transported from afar.

THE SOIL OF A BOUGHT BONSAI

When you acquire a mature bonsai, it's advisable to monitor the soil's moisture-holding capacity very carefully. If you buy a tree from a reputable grower, you should have at least a year before you need to replace the soil. Be watchful if you dramatically change the plant's environment. Say you live in a cold climate and buy a tree from a vendor located in a hot, sunny climate where trees are grown outdoors all year long. The tree may be planted in very moisture-retentive soil. When you move such a tree to an indoor environment with much less light, less ventilation, and stable temperatures,  it will take days and sometimes weeks for the soil to dry out, and the tree may succumb to root rot (which has happened to the best of us). If you notice that the tree stays wet longer than 36 hours, repot it into a more suitable soil as soon as possible.

Bonsai are easiest to grow in pots that are about two-thirds the length of the tree's height and filled half with roots and half with soil at the time of repotting.

A VITAL CONNECTION: SOIL MOISTURE, AERATION, AND CONTAINER SHAPE AND SIZE

Each and every soil blend varies in its ability to hold moisture, so you may have to adjust your watering schedule whenever you change the composition of the soil. In addition to the soil blend, the size and shape of the bonsai container determine how long the soil stays moist and whether there's enough air space for the roots to thrive. Here are a few general guidelines for creating a successful relationship between soil moisture retention, aeration, and container type. (For tips on picking the right-size pot for your tree, see page 96.)

- **Large Containers** Pots containing more than a quart or so of soil require large particle sizes ($1/8$ to $3/8$ inch) to maintain good aeration.

- **Small Containers** Pots that hold less than a quart of soil need finer soil mixes ($1/8$ inch and finer) to retain adequate moisture and yet remain porous enough to maintain adequate aeration.

- **Tiny Containers** Really small containers that hold less than a cup or two of soil mix dry out extremely fast and need to be checked frequently, at least twice daily.

- **Shallow Containers** Growing bonsai in shallow pots may be more difficult because it can be tricky to time watering. Initially upon being watered, a shallow pot holds more moisture (and less air) in its soil relative to the same volume of soil in a deeper pot. But it subsequently dries out faster because it has a larger surface area exposed to the air.

- **Deeper Containers** Bonsai growing is easier when pots retain more water at the bottom of the container while drying out faster near the top. A deeper container holds more air and less water than a shallow one.

- **Oversize Containers** It is also quite possible to plant a tree in a pot that's just too large for it. In that case the soil will be sodden and soggy (and virtually airless): There is too much soil mass and too few roots to absorb the moisture. Root rot will ensue. Move the tree to a smaller container as soon as possible.

- **Tricky Containers** Beginning growers should avoid growing trees in containers less than two inches deep or less than six to seven inches long, since these are the most difficult to water properly. Experienced growers who encounter problems with a specific tree often find that repotting a stressed tree into a somewhat larger and deeper container dramatically improves its health and vigor.

To help you visualize how soil depth, volume, and surface area relate to moisture retention, envision a rectangular sponge that is saturated with water and lying on a screen. When it lies on the screen with its largest surface facing down it soon stops dripping water. Lift it up so that it is now on its side, a deeper dimension: More water drips out. Now stand it upright: It drains yet more water. Applied to the soil in your bonsai pot, a deeper soil column holds less water and more air than a shallow container holding the same volume of soil.

Very shallow pots are difficult to water properly. They hold lots of moisture initially and then dry out rapidly.

Repotting and Root Pruning

Depending on tree species, growth pattern, and soil composition, bonsai need to be repotted and root pruned at one- to three-year intervals. Rapidly growing species like figs (*Ficus* species) may need to be repotted every year while slower-growing trees such as black olive (*Bucida molinetii*) may do well for three to five years in the same soil. In general, older and more mature bonsai require less frequent repotting because they grow more slowly than young trees and do not become root-bound as quickly as young trees. Maintaining a growing tree in the same size container for an indefinite period of time is one of the secrets of bonsai cultivation. The trick, of course, is to remove just the right amount of roots every time the tree is repotted, and that requires a delicate balancing act. Remove too much of the root mass and the tree dies, as it is unable to absorb enough water to keep adequately hydrated. Remove too little, and the roots grow longer and longer and the bonsai will need to be moved to a larger container. A reasonable root pruning removes 20 to 30 percent of the finer root hairs. Unless you are an experienced grower, it's best to follow this rule of thumb.

Step-by-Step Instructions

For most tropical bonsai the best time to repot is during the middle of their growth period. This often falls in early to midsummer. For subtropical species the best time to repot is spring, before new growth starts.

Due to the small size of their containers, bonsai need to be repotted often. Roots circling the soil perimeter are usually a sign that it's time to repot.

1. **Move the tree to an area away from direct sunlight and drying wind.** Keep a water-filled spray bottle at the ready so you can spray the roots as needed to keep them from drying out during repotting.

Use a butter knife or similar tool to loosen the soil around the pot margins.

2. **Check to see if the bonsai needs repotting.** Remove any retention wires holding the tree in the pot, then loosen the soil around the pot margins with a butter knife or similar tool. Gently lift the tree out of its container, holding it by its upper branches or upper foliage mass, and examine the roots. Never handle a rough- or shaggy-barked bonsai by the trunk, or its aged bark may fall away in your fingers, ruining many years of aged appearance. If roots are circling the soil perimeter and the soil does not fall away from the root ball, it is time to repot. If the soil crumbles away from the roots with little or no prodding, the bonsai can grow in the same soil for another year. Gently replace the tree in its container, backfill the soil into the pot, and secure the tree with a retention wire.

3. **If the bonsai requires repotting, remove the loosened tree from its pot.** Place it on a table or workbench covered with newspaper. Have fresh potting mix, wire, and clippers at the ready. While you are working, mist the roots with water as needed to keep them moist.

4. **Remove all old soil.** Using a pencil, chopstick, or small sharpened wooden dowel, penetrate the root ball near the trunk and gently ease your soil stick to the outside of the root ball. Repeat this as many times as necessary to remove most of the old soil and gently comb out the roots. Be sure to gently remove any clumps of clayey old soil adhering to the roots and especially any material attached to the base of the trunk. This material can easily cause rotting. Remember to keep the roots moist at all times during this process, misting them with water from the spray bottle.

5. **Trim back the longest woody roots.** Once all the soil has been removed, use pruners to shorten the woody roots—you can generally cut them back by a third of their length without harming the tree. Try to leave some of the hairy or fine "feeder" roots on the ends of the shortened woody roots.

Remove most old soil from the root ball. Use a pointed stick to tease the roots apart, inserting your tool in the soil near the trunk and easing it to the outside of the root ball.

6. **Remove part of the fibrous root mass.** For most healthy bonsai, it is safe and even necessary to remove about a third of the fibrous root mass when the tree is root-bound. To remove more mass, you need to know how tolerant your tree is of root removal, which you will learn with experience. At any rate, retain as many as possible of the fine hairlike roots that grow at the ends of the woody roots. You can remove woody structural roots that contain no root hairs with little ill effect. Woody roots are mostly there to support the tree and are not directly involved in moisture and nutrient absorption.

7. **Place a piece of screening over the empty pot's drain hole(s).** To keep soil from hampering drainage, use ¼-inch-mesh galvanized hardware cloth for larger pots and window screen for smaller pots (six inches long or less). A used pot does not need to be cleaned or disinfected unless it held a diseased tree. If necessary, disinfect the pot by soaking it in a 10 percent bleach solution for an hour or two. Before planting a tree in a disinfected pot, soak it in fresh water for a day or two to remove any residual bleach.

8. **Thread a retention wire through the drain hole(s).** Make sure the wire is long enough to reach from the drain hole all the way around the root ball and

MOVING A BONSAI INTO ITS FIRST POT

A tree being moved to a bonsai pot for the first time should have no more than one-third of its fine roots removed and thus may require a larger pot initially. After a year or two, the tree can be more vigorously root-pruned and moved into a smaller pot. Painstaking though it is, it's better to reduce your bonsai's root—and pot—size over time rather than skip steps and risk killing the tree.

Trim back the longest woody roots and remove part of the fibrous root mass. For most trees, it's safe to cut woody roots by a third and take off a third of the fibrous root mass.

up around the tree's trunk or main surface. The retention wire should be about pencil-lead thickness and made from aluminum.

9. **Set the tree back into its pot and spread out the roots.** The roots should take up about half the space in the pot.

10. **Add new, dry bonsai soil to the pot.** Settle it in around the roots with a gentle rotary movement of your soil stick. Avoid packing the soil in with jabbing movements. Add only enough soil so that its surface reaches just below the rim of the pot. Remember to keep the base of the trunk slightly above the pot's rim.

11. **Fasten the retention wire into place.** Use a protective bolster (such as a piece of tire rubber or inner tube) with the wire to hold the tree in place and to protect the roots and the tree's bark. Keep the wire in place until new roots have anchored the tree into its container. This usually takes about four to six weeks.

12. **Water the newly repotted tree immediately.** Use a basin of water in which to settle the potted tree to near the pot's rim, and allow it to sit for half an hour, or until the root ball is thoroughly soaked. Then remove the pot from the basin and allow the excess water to drain. Allow the soil to dry out somewhat before watering again. Newly repotted roots are very susceptible to root rot from excess moisture.

Post-Potting Procedures

Remove some of the leaf mass. Healthy trees maintain a balance between leaf mass and root mass. In most cases, when you've removed a portion of a plant's feeder roots at the time of repotting, it's a good idea to remove a similar percentage of leaves. Foliage is most easily removed by snipping off a leaf and leaving a small piece

Thread a retention wire through the drain holes, making sure it's long enough to reach from the holes all the way around the root ball and around the trunk.

of the leaf stem, or petiole, behind. The petiole will fall off in a week or two. Leaves may be removed from any area of the tree, but since the top of the tree is often more vigorous than the lower portions of the tree, the apex of the tree can usually tolerate a higher percentage of leaf removal. (See page 20 for more on leaf pruning.)

Keep the tree out of direct sunlight and wind for a week after repotting. Gradually move the tree back to its normal growing spot over the following week or two. Start fertilizing two to three weeks after repotting. Once the tree has grown five or more leaves at each growing point, you can consider trimming or wiring the tree for shape.

Once the tree is stable, you can cut the retention wire. After four to six weeks, check to see if the tree is stable by loosening the wire and trying to wiggle the trunk. If the roots have grown properly, the tree will be secure in its container. Snip the wire at the soil surface and unwire the top portion from the bonsai. Gently pull the lower portion out from the bottom of the pot.

THE RIGHT POT FOR THE TREE

Bonsai pots are available at most garden centers. Before purchasing a pot be sure to take a look inside: It should never be glazed and the bottom should have one or more holes that allow for proper drainage. When choosing a container pick one whose length is two thirds the height of the tree and that can hold about the same soil volume as the canopy. Some plants like a drier soil environment, and these will do better in a pot containing a smaller soil volume. Plants that like a wetter soil will do better in a somewhat larger pot.

Set the tree into the pot and spread out its roots. Add new sifted bonsai soil to the pot and settle it in around the root ball with your stick. Then secure the retention wire.

If the tree is still loose, leave the wire in place for another month before testing again. Also leave the retention wire in place if you plan to move your tree outside for the summer. It can help keep the tree anchored if it gets knocked over by a strong wind or a rambunctious pet. Check periodically to make sure that the wire is not cutting into the bark.

Willow-leaf fig just after repotting. Prune out a similar percentage of foliage as the amount of fine roots that were removed.

Adequate lighting is key to healthy plant growth. If natural light is too dim or unavailable, choose artificial plant lights to supplement it.

Natural and Artificial Lighting

Providing adequate amounts of light is essential for the long-term well-being of bonsai cultivated indoors. If the growing area is too dim, many trees will compensate by making larger leaves and producing leggy growth in order to capture the necessary amount of light to survive and grow—a natural response of the tree, but not part of the plan of the bonsai grower.

Low Light, Medium Light, Bright Light In general, trees belong in one of three broad categories. They may require low light, the amount of light in a room with just enough light by which to read newsprint; medium light, light from a south or west window on a sunny spring day; or bright light, the amount of light outdoors on a clear summer day.

Reflective Materials A simple way to increase available light from any source is to use reflective materials around and underneath your bonsai. Plain white cardboard or Mylar sheets placed around and under the bonsai reflect light back to the tree. The drawback is that these types of reflectors may not be particularly attractive in a home environment. Painting the walls white in the growing area may be a more subtle option that also significantly increases available light.

Natural Lighting: Windowsill Growing

A south- or west-facing window is best for bonsai culture. This position provides adequate light for species with low to medium light requirements—most of the species covered in this book. Generally, north- and east-facing windows do not provide enough light to keep plants healthy.

Turning Trees When growing one or more bonsai on a windowsill, turn each tree so that every side is exposed to full light from time to time. If trees are not turned regularly, they will have fewer leaves and weaker branches on the side facing away from the window and will start to look lopsided. Consider turning trees that grow on a windowsill a quarter turn every week.

Curtain Concerns If the window is curtained, bear in mind that airy fabric, which allows the room temperature to moderate the windowsill's temperature, is much safer for your trees than thermal or heavy fabric, which insulates the plants from the air in the room. Insulated by heavy curtains, bonsai may easily overheat on warm sunny days and get chilled during cold winter nights.

Watering Concerns Also note that the watering needs of windowsill specimens will vary greatly depending on light exposure, time of year, and weather. Trees in small pots, for example, may need to be watered more than once a day when it's sunny. Be vigilant and check your plants frequently.

Artificial Lighting: Color, Intensity, Duration

If natural light is too dim or unavailable, artificial lights are a useful alternative. In addition to overhead lighting, arrange some lamps at the sides of the trees to help the lower limbs get adequate light. If artificial light is only directed from the top of the tree, lower limbs will weaken over time and the top branches will become too heavy. Some growers rig lights on chains and tip them over to light the sides of the tree. Others use a floor lamp to direct light from the sides.

Light Color Plants don't use all light frequencies equally but best absorb light in the blue and red spectrums. (Plants do not use the green light frequency effectively, and it is reflected away—that's why plants look green.) Blue light frequencies are used mainly for vegetative growth, the formation and elongation of stems, leaves, and roots—the main concern for bonsai cultivation. The use of bulbs emitting light mainly in the blue range fosters good plant growth with moderate fruiting and flowering. Red light frequencies are used by plants for fruit and flower formation. The use of bulbs emitting red frequencies triggers bonsai to spend a lot of energy on making flowers and fruit—which can actually weaken the tree. For long-term success, use mainly blue frequencies with a little red.

Light Intensity Physics teaches us that light energy decreases with the square of the distance from the light source. A plant at a distance of two feet from a light source receives one quarter of the emitted light energy received by a plant at one foot. More simply put, plants should be as close as safely possible to the light source. Beware of the heat emitted by some types of artificial lighting.

Light Duration The total light energy that plants absorb is a factor of light frequency (spectrum), light intensity, and day length. So the more time plants are exposed to light, the more energy they will absorb. It is not known if some plants actually require a rest period, but keeping lights on around the clock is probably not a good idea. Most indoor growers using artificial light have a 12- to 18-hour day length set with a simple clock timer. Experiment with your grow-lights to determine your plants' optimum day length. Remember also that some plants key their growth or flowering to the length of day or night. Hibiscuses, for instance, flower in the shortening days of fall, while most azaleas bloom in spring. Other plants like serissa bloom nearly continuously, regardless of day length.

Artificial Lights: The Most Common Options
Fluorescent Lights

Fluorescent lights are a useful option that allows you to grow a greater variety of plants than you can grow with the natural light available on a windowsill. Fluorescents use relatively little electricity and are quite low in light output, so plants must be very close to them. That's not a problem, since plants can be almost touching a fluorescent bulb without burning the leaves. Cool white bulbs alone or a mix of warm white and cool white fluorescent bulbs work quite well for many bonsai. The ends of the fluorescent bulbs emit much less energy than the center, so it is important to rotate trees to allow them to benefit from the extra energy at the bulb's center. Move the trees from the center of the bulb to the end on a monthly rotation. Bulbs should be replaced as recommended on the bulb label. In comparison, fluorescents produce light with much less energy than metal halide lights and generate much less waste heat.

High-Intensity-Discharge Systems

High-intensity-discharge lights promote superb growth and flowering, allowing cultivation of trees that require plenty of bright light. Plants will actually grow significantly and increase their girth and leaf density when cultivated under metal halide lamps. These same plants would appear almost static and not show any real increase in size or branching under moderate- to low-light conditions.

Metal halide lamps, the most common HID lights, are efficient in converting electricity to light. Metal halides provide high light output with relatively high efficiency. Fixtures come in many sizes, shapes, and types, commonly available from 50 watts to

1,500 watts. The higher the wattage, the larger the area under which plants can be grown. A 400-watt lamp can adequately light an area of approximately four by four feet, a 1,000-watt lamp an area of six by six feet. Metal halides work well for trees that require plenty of bright light.

There are a few drawbacks, however. Each metal halide light comes with a transformer that can usually handle only one lamp and is suitable only for the wattage for which it is built. In other words, if you have a 250-watt transformer, you cannot upgrade to a 1,000-watt lamp later on. Neither lamps nor transformers may get wet. The transformers produce a humming sound, which can be annoying in a quiet home. In addition, metal halide lamps produce significant heat; the tops of trees must be kept at least one foot from the lamps or the closest leaves will burn. It is possible, however, to reduce the risk of leaf burn by improving ventilation.

Sodium lamps, another type of light source, are not recommended for bonsai. The yellow-color light they emit gives the plants a peculiar appearance and, more importantly, fosters stem elongation (etiolation), which is not desirable.

Some of these leaves were scorched by grow-lights that were suspended too close to the top of the tree. Be sure to check how hot your lights get and keep trees at a safe distance.

LED Lights

LEDs are the most recent addition to the world of plant lights. The tiny devices were once limited to use in computers and other electronic devices but are now finding more applications in the commercial sector. They are more expensive to purchase than other plant lighting options, but they are very energy efficient. Over a number of years, the higher initial cost of LED bulbs will be offset by lower electricity bills.

LED plant lights are outfitted with collections of individual red, blue, and orange bulbs, and their correct placement is vital for success with bonsai. The relatively low-powered bulbs must be kept fairly close to the plants, but if they are too close to the foliage, the various light spectra may not be mixed efficiently, and plant leaves may get overexposed to light of one frequency. Follow manufacturer's recommendations to optimize the distance between light and plant. These bulbs don't produce heat, so the need for ventilation and cooling is greatly reduced. In my personal experience with them, however, I have found that LEDs are not as effective as simple fluorescent fixtures for successfully growing many indoor bonsai.

Not for Bonsai: Incandescent Bulbs and Halogen Bulbs

Incandescent bulbs, the typical lighting still found in most homes, is not recommended for home bonsai growing. Incandescents produce light mainly in the red frequencies and are deficient in the blue frequencies needed by plants. They are also inefficient in producing light energy, as much of the electricity is spent on producing heat, requiring that plants be at some distance from the bulbs to avoid burning.

Halogen lighting is also inefficient in producing light because so much of the electrical power goes toward producing heat. As with incandescent bulbs, plants need to be some distance from the light to avoid being burned. For indoor bonsai, halogen lights are not suitable.

The Best Lighting Types at a Glance

TYPE OF LIGHT	LIGHT OUTPUT	ELECTRICITY COSTS	PURCHASE PRICE	ADVANTAGES	DISADVANTAGES
Fluorescent	Low	Moderate–low	Low	Low cost, cool	Low light output
Metal halide	High	High	High	Efficient	High costs, high heat output
LED	Moderate	Low	Very high	Efficient	High initial cost

SUMMERING BONSAI OUTDOORS

Many bonsai growers move their trees outdoors during the warm summer weather. This has many advantages: Outdoors, plants are exposed to good humidity, excellent air circulation, and real sunlight. Often the trees show significant growth only during the time they spend outdoors. Once they return to the less hospitable indoor environment, they usually enter a rest period and often lose many of their leaves. In a sense, the time spent indoors during the colder months is just a holding period that tides the trees over until they are back outdoors the following summer.

There are, of course, disadvantages to rotating bonsai indoors and out: Trees are exposed to insects, marauding wildlife, the vagaries of weather and fluctuating temperatures, and they may get stolen or vandalized.

Moving trees from indoors to outdoors requires a gradual transition to give the trees time to adapt to the stronger outdoor light. Leaves that have grown indoors do not tolerate strong sunlight. They must be allowed to gradually adapt to brighter light. Move the indoor tree outside to dappled shade, and each week increase its sun exposure by an hour or two. After a month it is safe to expose the tree to full sun for about half a day. Move the tree to dappled sunlight for the remainder of the day. Be extra vigilant about watering: A tree's needs increase dramatically once it is in sunlight and outside air. If the bonsai container is small, you may have to water two or more times daily. Very small pots can be particularly impractical for outdoor exposure. Set the small pots in moist sand that comes up to their rim, and keep them in filtered sun at all times. Water the bonsai soil and the surrounding sand as needed.

It's time to move tropical bonsai back indoors when nighttime temperatures drop to around 55°F in late summer or fall. In the preceding month, reverse the transition procedure you followed in spring. Move the trees to increasing shade. It will make the change to indoor living more successful, and the trees will shed many fewer leaves.

Some subtropical trees may benefit from staying outside until nighttime temperatures are near freezing.

Carefully examine all plants before moving them back indoors and treat any insect infestations beforehand.

Many trees benefit from time spent outdoors; they thrive in sunlight, gentle breezes, and light rain.

Starting bonsai from seed requires patience, but some trees, like tamarind or kumquat, for example, can grow into a respectable tree within five to ten years.

Starting Your Own Bonsai: Seeds, Cuttings, Air Layers, and Nursery Stock

Robert Mahler

Starting your own bonsai is, of course, much less costly than purchasing a mature specimen, and it is an excellent way to develop a sense for the patterns of tree growth and the techniques of bonsai training. There are four ways to start your own bonsai: by seed, cutting, air layer, and nursery stock. Each has its advantages and drawbacks, and all require a good dose of patience. What follows is a brief overview of the basic steps to get a tree started using each of the four methods.

Starting from Seed

Not surprisingly, the least expensive route takes the most time. Your endurance will be rewarded with a bonsai that is superior in shape as well as root structure because you have control of the tree's form by wiring and judicious root pruning from the very beginning. Start seeds for bonsai as you would any others indoors. Before you plant, check whether it is advisable to soak them in water or nick the seed coats first. Fill a shallow nursery tray with a seed-starting mix. Place the seeds one to two inches apart, cover them with soil and gently tamp it down, and thoroughly water. Place the tray in an area with southern or western sun exposure and keep the seedbed evenly moist. Spring or early summer is the best time to start seeds with natural light. Alternatively, place the seeds under a grow-light suspended approximately three to four inches from the top of the soil. Depending on the plant species, your seeds should sprout within a week or two. Once the seedlings have grown two sets of leaves in addition to the seed leaves, you can move them to small individual pots. As soon as your trees start showing woody growth, start guiding the developing trunk and branches with wires.

Cuttings

Trees grown from cuttings develop good root structure and can be wired at a young age, which gets them off to a good start as bonsai. A cutting may develop roots very easily or much less so—it all depends on the species. To improve your chances, buy rooting hormone and cutting soil mix (if possible, one specifically recommended for your plant). To take the cutting, choose a branch that's three to four inches long, shows good lateral branching, and mirrors a small to medium bonsai in size. Make the cut at an angle, immediately below a node bud. Fill a small pot with cutting mix, packing down the soil. Use a dibble or small stick to make a hole in the soil, dip the cut end of the branch into the rooting hormone, and place the cutting into the hole. Pack the

soil firmly around the cutting and moisten the soil. Place a tent over the cutting (a clear plastic bag will do), and move it to an area with good southern or western sun exposure. If you use grow-lights, place them three to four inches above the top of the plastic bag. Keep the soil evenly moist. Roots should emerge within one to four weeks. Once the new tree has developed a good root system, you can move it to a bonsai pot and start working on it.

A tamarind seedling six years after germination is ten inches tall and well on its way to becoming a vigorous bonsai.

Air layering step by step: Strip the bark of the cambium layer in a circle around the branch. Apply a thick layer of New Zealand sphagnum peat moss and wrap the whole in clear plastic. Once roots have formed, remove the branch from the tree. Unwrap the air layer and plant it.

Air Layers

Simply put, an air layer is a rooted branch. The technique allows you to create a more mature plant with a well-developed trunk in a relatively short time. Scout a tree for a branch that resembles a small to medium bonsai. Good branching is a must. Take special note of the placement of the first, second, and third branch (from the bottom). Once you've settled on a branch that suits you, strip the bark to the cambium layer in the area where you want the bonsai to develop roots. Work in a circle around the branch. Apply damp New Zealand sphagnum moss in a thick layer over the stripped area and wrap the whole in clear plastic. Keep the area evenly moist until roots emerge. Water with a syringe or keep a section of the plastic open and water with a can. Either way, do not overwater the air layer—too much can promote rot. Once roots are visible through the plastic, remove the air layer by cutting the branch off below the new root mass, unwrap it, and plant it in a small pot. Keep the newly rooted plant out of direct sunlight until new growth emerges.

Nursery Stock

Tropical, subtropical, and warm-temperate plants can be obtained from nurseries on the East Coast and in Canada in late spring and summer. They are readily available year-round in the southern and western parts of the United States. Look for a strong-growing healthy plant that has many low branches. The trunk flare should be visible and well developed, and the trunk itself should be thickest at the base so that it can develop good taper over time. Choose the branches you want to keep, wire them as needed, and trim back wayward growth. Then take the tree out of its nursery pot and cut back the root system. You can safely remove up to a third of the root mass to fit the tree into its first bonsai pot, which should be filled with about equal parts roots and soil.

Due to its dense branching pattern, this nursery plant offers many options for training. The disproportionately hefty branch on the left is removed first. Then the remaining branches are assessed for their position and diameter and either pruned out or shortened and wired so they can be eased into place and gently bent to work toward a natural-looking curvature.

Bonsai Health Care

James F. and Mary Kay Doyle

Whether you acquire your indoor bonsai from a friend, from a reputable nursery, through trading with bonsai aficionados, or as a surprise from the bonsai fairy, you should get as much information as you can about where and how your plant grows in nature. In order to create favorable indoor growing conditions, you need to know a plant's preferences for temperature, light, moisture, and soil. Based on the information you gather, you can adapt the environment in which your plant grows and create conditions that are close to those found in the plant's native habitat. In that way you are doing your best to assure that your plant stays strong and thrives.

Keeping your plant healthy goes a long way toward keeping pests and diseases at bay. Most of the time, an insect pest or a disease will attack a weak or stressed plant before a healthy one, so step one in pest and disease management is maintaining the health of your bonsai. In the event of an infestation, a healthy tree is also much better able to fend off the attackers than a tree whose health has been compromised by poor living conditions.

Plant Health Tips

Choose plants suited to your growing conditions. The indoor plant environment can be fine-tuned with the help of artificial lights, heaters, humidity trays, and fans. It's up to you to decide how much you want to take on. You'll also learn that some plants can do well with your degree of attentiveness and some cannot. If a plant fails despite your best efforts, don't take it personally, and don't beat a dead horse (or plant). That being said, don't allow your plant to perish in vain: You should be able to learn something when a tree dies.

Monitor the health of your plants. Daily care, at least in the introductory phase, allows you to monitor conditions closely and make timely adjustments. Note any changes in your plant and its environment. Recognizing signs of plant stress or pest infestation can give you valuable clues to the most suitable response. Outdoor conditions also have an effect on your indoor plants. Changes in day length and weather patterns, for example, affect the amount of water they require day to day.

Provide the right amount of light. An ideal indoor location should offer consistent light—natural, artificial, or a combination that is appropriate for the needs of the particular plant. For example, the light that comes in through a bright southern or western window might be enough to keep a tree that needs very bright light alive, whereas a "day length" extended to 12 to 14 hours with the help of grow-lights might actually help it to grow.

Provide ventilation. Air circulation provided by an oscillating fan can help moderate temperature extremes and prevent the growth of mold and mildew. It also causes the plant to take up more water and promotes the drying of the soil.

Beware of too much or too little water. Water, or the lack of it, is the primary cause of plant death in bonsai. Underwatering generally causes the wilting of leaves first and then affects the branches. If a plant doesn't have enough moisture to maintain all its foliage, it will first drop older leaves (those growing closer to the base of a branch). Overwatering causes problems in the root zone. The signs of root damage may appear as wilting, browning, or distortion of the leaves at the growing tips or as random branch dieback.

Strive for balance between great design and plant health. Some of us are better stylists than caretakers. Remember, a poorly styled live tree is better than an exquisitely styled dead one. Don't sacrifice the health of a tree to the glory of design. Use restraint. Patience, above all, may be what bonsai lovers learn from these little trees.

Maintain good sanitation. Keep the plant pot free of debris like dead leaves and blooms, which could harbor insect hatchlings and promote diseases. Keep weeds, moss, and groundcovers from growing up the trunk of the tree.

Look for yellowing leaves. Mineral deficiencies can cause a general yellowing of the foliage or along the leaf veins. They may be linked to the pH of your water or the balance of the soil components. Intermittent use of a fertilizer with trace elements can help alleviate the problem and help the plants to access nutrients.

Check for black spot and powdery mildew. Both are fungal in origin. Remove marked or damaged leaves and keep dead foliage off the soil surface. Avoid watering the foliage; unless it evaporates quickly, water on leaves can invite fungal infection. Increase air circulation, which can help prevent conditions conducive to fungi growth (in part because it forces the plants to use more moisture).

Give your plants some fresh air. Most bonsai benefit from time outdoors in the warm weather; trees thrive in natural sunlight with a light breeze and gentle rain. Before moving the plants back indoors, check them closely for insects, or better still, make the change over a week or two, keeping each plant temporarily in isolation from the others and examining it frequently.

Washing your plants with a watering can or with a garden hose outfitted with a gentle nozzle is a good way to clean off dust, pollutants, and pests. Do it on a warm, breezy day so the water evaporates quickly. Do not mist plants. Misting traps pollutants and dust and blocks sunlight.

Insect Plant Pests

Check for signs of insect infestation. Harmful insects (some of which carry plant diseases too) may hatch, walk in, fly in, hitch a ride in on you or your pet, blow in through a ventilation system, or be introduced through contact with an infected plant. If a plant appears "unhappy," inspect it closely and try to identify the problem as soon as you can.

Catching insect pests in the early stages of infestation is very important to limit the extent of the damage. An inexpensive magnifying lens with a light is helpful for zeroing in on culprits. When you find a pest has taken up residence on a plant, isolate the pot from your other plants to keep the problem from spreading.

Many insects hide, feed, mate, and lay eggs on the underside of leaves. Others may be found nestled in tender new growth where they feed. There are also those that camouflage themselves along the trunk or in the bark and in branch unions. Familiarize yourself with the most common plant pests below and examine your plants carefully on a regular basis.

Aphids generally gravitate to the succulent new growth on plants. These soft-bodied insects may be light green to black. If you see ants running along the trunk of a tree, check for aphids—ants feed on the sugary residue (honeydew) that the aphids produce.

Fungus gnats are black flies, smaller than fruit flies, that harbor in overly moist soil. The first response is to allow the soil to dry between waterings, which hinders the larvae from hatching.

Mealybugs are often identified by the cottony white masses that accumulate in the whorls of new unfurling leaves and at junctures of leaf stems and branches. The cottony white material protects the eggs. Adult individuals have ovate white bodies and are found on leaves, stems, roots, and flowers—they may also hide on the bottom of the pot.

Scales have armored shells cupped over their vulnerable insect bodies. The young crawlers hatched under that protective shell move out along the trunk and woody branches to find succulent tissue where they can settle in and start sucking sap. The telltale sign of scale infestation is a sticky residue on the leaves. If you notice a sticky substance on the tabletop below a tree, check the branches and leaves immediately above it. Chances are you'll find scale insects.

Spider mites are almost imperceptible to the naked eye, and their presence may only be detected by the damage they do. Leaf surfaces appear stippled or dusty and bleached of color. The mites feed and breed on the underside of leaves; try flicking a leaf or branch over a white sheet of paper and look for any dark specks that move. An advanced colony may form webbing among the tree's branch tips, which becomes more visible when you spray it with one of the controls on the list that follows.

Whiteflies are pretty easy to identify. Make any movement near the plant, and they take to the air like tiny snowflakes. They generally lay their eggs on the underside of leaves and prefer soft fleshy growth from which to suck sap. Their ability to fly can make containing an infestation challenging.

Least-Toxic Pest Controls

Beyond monitoring the physical environment of your plants, which is your first line of defense, try these methods to control pests on indoor bonsai. They are the least toxic for you, your plants, and the environment you share with the other members of your household. Mix up a quart-size bottle of one of the general controls listed below, following the manufacturer's recommendations. Treat the infested plant on a seven- to ten-day cycle until you are sure that no further generations of the pest have hatched. Be sure to treat the tops as well as the undersides of leaves, where many pests live or hide. When you have finished the spray, switch to something else on the list. That way you avoid promoting the development of resistant strains of pests. Always check the label for plants to avoid, and test the spray on a few leaves before applying it to delicate foliage.

General Controls

Horticultural oil applied by thorough spraying can suffocate insects and subdue the spread of fungal spores. Lightweight horticultural oils that evaporate quickly can be safely used on actively growing plants. Avoid repeated applications of oil in a humid environment. An accumulation of oil can suffocate plant foliage.

Neem oil has the general suffocating effect of horticultural oils, but it also contains insecticidal and fungicidal compounds. It has a garlicky scent that dissipates within

Insect pests in close-up view from top to bottom: aphid, fungus gnat, mealybugs, scales, spider mite, and whiteflies.

a day or two after spraying. It is effective against most soft-bodied insects, armored scales, and some fungi.

Insecticidal soap contains potassium salts of fatty acids. A thorough spraying effectively kills most pests on contact. Do not use the soap in direct sun or heat, because it may burn the foliage. Time the application for a cloudy day or wait until the sun has set.

Soap and alcohol are good complements to your insect-control regimen and are readily available in most households. A capful of rubbing alcohol and a small squirt of a mild detergent (half a teaspoon) in a quart spray bottle of water is particularly helpful in cleaning up the sticky residue of scale, as well as in controlling the insect. Soap and alcohol may also be applied by using two clean sponges dipped in the diluted solution to wipe the top and bottom leaf surfaces at the same time. Rubbing alcohol may be applied directly to insects with a cotton swab, but it can be damaging to plants' delicate growing tips.

Yellow sticky cards—which are exactly what they sound like—are helpful in monitoring and trapping flying insects like whiteflies and fungus gnats, which can be difficult to affect with a spray. The cards, suspended a few inches above the bonsai, can also help prevent the spread of an infestation while you gain control of additional larval hatchings.

Specific Controls

Gnatrol is a product developed to control fungus gnats. A drench of Bti (*Bacillus thuringiensis israelensis*), it is effective in killing the larvae in the soil. The product remains in the soil for about 48 hours. It takes about two or three drenchings to get all the hatches in an infestation.

Flea collars can be helpful to control some insects that bore into the plant or live in dense foliage where spraying is dif-

Inspect your trees regularly for signs of pest infestation. The earlier you detect a problem the easier it is to manage.

ficult. Place the infected plant in a clear plastic bag with an activated flea collar and keep it out of direct sunlight for 24 hours. Repeat again in 10 to 14 days to fumigate subsequent hatchings. This is a chemical control. The risk to the environment and the applicator is reduced through containment.

Protekt is a silica product from Dyna Gro that can be included in a fertilizer regimen. It builds up in the vascular systems of the plant to prevent desiccation and wilting due to heat stress and drought. It also helps build stronger cell walls that are more resistant to insect attacks.

Pyrethrins are plant-derived insecticides. They are contact poisons and may be effective for particularly persistent infestations. Pyrethrins are safe for use around mammals and birds but are lethal to fish and crustaceans.

Integrated pest management (IPM) is an approach to pest control that includes the introduction of predators, such as ladybugs, beneficial aphids, and mites, to feed on specific pest populations. This practice is most effective for a particular outbreak in a greenhouse or atrium environment. It would be inappropriate in many home environments. Seek the advice of a source hatchery to find out which insects would be most effective in your situation.

Other Pesky Critters

Slugs and snails can be a problem in high-humidity environments or in a summer location outdoors. Their glistening trail of slime should lead you to look under the pot or bench. After removing the ones you find, set out shallow trays of beer to attract and drown the craftier ones. In a greenhouse environment, a toad is a friendly predator with a big appetite. Just as for insects, check your plants thoroughly when moving them indoors.

Cats and dogs extend their territory indoors. Refrain from using a fertilizer if you discover your pet likes the smell or taste of it. Neem oil smells garlicky and may discourage a cat that likes to chomp on plant foliage or a dog that finds a bonsai makes a nice retrieving stick.

Birds, rodents, and deer are only a threat outdoors. There is always some new gimmick you can try to baffle them. Cutout images or silhouettes of cats can be a great help in keeping birds at bay. Fake snakes and owls fool most ornery critters at least some of the time. Bars of strong-scented deodorant soap near your trees may discourage rodents and deer. If you have a lily pond or other water feature, a pump-powered bamboo deer chaser—which makes a clacking noise at irregular intervals—may scare away interlopers. The most effective all-purpose deterrent to date may be a motion-sensing sprinkler that goes into action when animals approach. If all else fails, you can set up barriers to prevent animal access and use aluminum foil to protect trunks from chewing damage.

For More Information

Bonsai Clubs and Societies

Most of these clubs have extensive reference lists on their websites of local, regional, and international clubs and societies. Local and regional groups are great resources to help you find vendors of good-quality bonsai in your area. The American Bonsai Society and Bonsai Clubs International also publish regular magazines, *Bonsai: Journal of the American Bonsai Society*, and *Bonsai Magazine*, respectively.

American Bonsai Society
absbonsai.org
(North America)

Bonsai Clubs International
bonsai-bci.com
(International focus on bonsai)

Bonsai Societies of Florida
bonsai-bsf.com
(Florida and Southeastern U.S.)

Golden State Bonsai Federation
gsbf-bonsai.org
(California)

National Bonsai Foundation
www.bonsai-nbf.org
(U.S. National Arboretum, Washington, DC)

Knowledge of Bonsai Forums
knowledgeofbonsai.org

NORTH AMERICAN BONSAI COLLECTIONS

Brooklyn Botanic Garden
1000 Washington Avenue
Brooklyn, NY 11225
718-623-7200
bbg.org

Chicago Botanic Garden
1000 Lake Cook Road
Glencoe, IL 60022
847-835-5440
chicagobotanic.org

GSBF Bonsai Garden at Lake Merritt
Lake Merritt Park
666 Bellevue Avenue
Oakland, CA 94601
510-763-8409
www.gsbf-bonsai.org/lake-merritt/
newhome.htm

GSBF Collection at the Huntington
Huntington Library and Botanical Gardens
1151 Oxford Road
San Marino, CA 91108
626-405-2100
www.gsbf-bonsai.org/huntington/
gsbfhuntwelcomenew.html

Montreal Botanic Garden
4101 Rue Sherbrooke Est
Montreal, Quebec
Canada H1X 2B2
514-872-1400
www2.ville.montreal.qc.ca/jardin/en/

Morikami Museum and Japanese Garden
4000 Morikami Park Road
Delray Beach, FL 33446
561-495-0233
morikami.org

National Bonsai & Penjing Museum
U.S. National Arboretum
3501 New York Avenue NE
Washington, DC 20002-1958
202-396-3510
www.bonsai-nbf.org

Pacific Rim Bonsai Collection
Weyerhaeuser Company
33663 Weyerhaeuser Way South
Federal Way, WA 98003
800-525-5440, ext. 5206
weyerhaeuser.com/bonsai

Contributors

James F. and Mary Kay Doyle own Nature's Way Nursery and Bonsai Studio in Harrisburg, Pennsylvania (natureswaybonsai.com). Their love of plants began with a landscaping business in 1973, which led them to the art of manipulation and pruning of tiny trees and all that goes with it. They credit bonsai with introducing them to an ever-widening group of similarly afflicted people around the planet. Their interest in an organic approach to living has led them toward earth- and people-friendly options for pest and disease control.

Pat Lucke Morris, a student of bonsai since 1974, has worked at a variety of jobs, including editor and graphic designer, before retiring from the workforce to spend her time on "important" pursuits such as bonsai. Pat has been an active member of the American Bonsai Society since 1985; she has served the ABS as a director and currently is its secretary. She is a past president and longtime member of the Brandywine Bonsai Society and also is a member of the Delaware Valley Bonsai Study Group and the Pennsylvania Bonsai Society.

Robert Mahler started his bonsai career at the age of 15. An apprenticeship under Chase Rosade of Rosade Bonsai Studio in New Hope, Pennsylvania, led to full-immersion study in Japan under the direction of the world-renowned bonsai master Susumo Sudo. Within a year of returning to the U.S., Robert was granted the position of curator of bonsai at Brooklyn Botanic Garden. Rob left the Garden in fall 2005 to pursue his own bonsai business (kifubonsai.com). He is fluent in Japanese and available for lectures, classes, and private tours abroad.

Jerry Meislik has been actively involved with bonsai for more than 30 years. He is particularly interested in tropical/indoor bonsai and plant material native to the U.S. He has authored two bonsai books: *Ficus: The Exotic Bonsai* and *Introduction to Indoor Bonsai*. He has held board positions in the American Bonsai Society and the National Bonsai Foundation and chaired the American Bonsai Society editorial board, in addition to serving as northwest editor of the North American Bonsai Federation website. Jerry teaches bonsai at Flathead Valley Community College, travels around the country teaching and lecturing about bonsai, and contributes articles to the major bonsai journals. Visit bonsaihunk.us to learn more.

Pauline F. Muth has been an ardent bonsai enthusiast for over three decades. She has been a member of her original club (Mohawk Hudson Bonsai Society in the capital district area of New York) for more than 25 years and now serves on the board of directors. Beyond her local affiliation, Pauline is active in many organizations and contributes to publications dealing with bonsai and the advancement of the art form. She is former president of the American Bonsai Society, secretary of Bonsai Clubs International, and on the board of directors of Mid-Atlantic Bonsai Societies. She is a contributing writer for local newsletters as well as *Bonsai Online Magazine, Bonsai: Journal of the American Bonsai Society,* and *Bonsai Magazine*. Pauline has also taught classes, workshops, and demonstrations in between owning and operating a bonsai teaching studio for over 18 years. She has also been the recipient of several local, regional, and international bonsai awards. More about Pauline and her work in bonsai can be found online at pfmbonsai.com.

Julian Velasco is curator of the bonsai collection and C.V. Starr Bonsai Museum at Brooklyn Botanic Garden. He began his bonsai studies with Chase Rosade of Rosade Bonsai Studio, then apprenticed with then bonsai curator Robert Mahler among Brooklyn Botanic Garden's world-renowned bonsai collection. Julian succeeded Robert as bonsai curator in the spring of 2006. His main interests are the philosophical and spiritual aspects of bonsai.

Sigrun Wolff Saphire was the senior editor of Brooklyn Botanic Garden's publications for ten years. She is currently a writer, curriculum developer, and consultant for urban gardening and environmental stewardship programs in New York City.

Photos

Karen Lynn Alstadt pages 56, 57 (bonsai by Lynn Perry)

Chicago Botanic Garden (Juliana Pino) pages 4, 15, 34, 35 (2), 54, 55, 60, 61, 62, 63 (2), 66, 67 (2), 70, 71 right, 76, 112

Jess Davis pages 25, 28

Elizabeth Ennis page 103

Jardin Botanique de Montréal (Michel Tremblay) pages 14, 16, 77

Jerry Meislik pages 26, 52 (2), 53, 58, 80, 83, 89, 90, 91, 92, 93, 94 (2), 95 (2), 96 (2), 97 (3), 98, 101, 104, 105, 106 (6)

U.S. National Arboretum pages 7, 11

Jerry Pavia pages 32 left, 59, 71 left, 79 right

Walter Pall pages 8, 30

Michael Ratliff cover

Neil Soderstrom pages 2, 12, 20, 22 (2), 23 (2), 24 (3), 27, 29, 32 right, 33, 36 (2), 37, 38, 39, 42, 43 (2), 46, 47, 48, 49, 50, 51 (2), 64 left, 65, 68 (2), 69, 72, 73, 74, 75 (2), 78, 79 left, 86, 88 (6), 107 (2) (bonsai at BBG, except pages 2, 72, 73: bonsai by Anthony Crupi)

Julian Velasco pages 44 (2), 45, 64 (right)

Pat and Chuck Ware pages 40, 41

Illustrations

Steve Buchanan plant pests, page 111

Elizabeth Ennis bonsai styles, page 11

Pauline F. Muth bonsai styles, except page 11

Index

PROVIDING EXPERT GARDENING ADVICE FOR OVER 60 YEARS

Join Brooklyn Botanic Garden as an annual Subscriber Member and have new gardening handbooks delivered directly to you, plus BBG newsletters, mailings, and privileges at many botanic gardens across the country. Visit bbg.org/subscribe for details.

BBG GUIDES FOR A GREENER PLANET

World renowned for pioneering gardening information, Brooklyn Botanic Garden's award-winning guides provide practical advice in a compact format for gardeners across North America. To order other fine titles, shop online at bbg.org/handbooks or call 718-623-7280. To learn more about Brooklyn Botanic Garden, visit bbg.org.